Baby Play

D1316134

Baby Play

Consulting Editors
Dr. Wendy S. Masi
Dr. Roni Cohen Leiderman

BARNES & NOBLE
NEW YORK

This edition published by Barnes & Noble, Inc., by arrangement with Weldon Owen Inc.

2004 Barnes & Noble Books
Copyright © 2004 Gym-Mark, Inc., and Weldon Owen Inc.
All rights reserved. Unauthorized reproduction, in any manner, is prohibited. Originally published in hardback in 1999.
10 9 8 7 6 5 4 3

Library of Congress Cataloging-in-Publication
data is available.
ISBN-10: 0-7607-5898-0
ISBN-13: 978-0-7607-5898-4
Printed in Singapore.

CONSULTING EDITORS

Dr. Wendy S. Masi
Dr. Roni Cohen Leiderman

GYMBOREE PLAY & MUSIC PROGRAMS

Chief Executive Officer: **Lisa Harper**
Vice President of Operations: **Donald Hendricks**
Product Manager: **Lisa Biasotti**
Play & Music Sr. Program Developer: **Helene Silver Freda**

WELDON OWEN INC.

Chief Executive Officer: **John Owen**
Chief Operating Officer & President: **Terry Newell**
Vice President & Publisher: **Roger Shaw**
Vice President, International Sales: **Stuart Laurence**

Publisher: **Rebecca Poole Forée**
Series Manager: **Brynn Breuner**
Managing Editors: **Elizabeth Dougherty, Jane B. Mason, Sarah Hines Stephens**
Author: **Susan Elisabeth Davis**
Copy Editors: **Peter Cieply, Kim Keller, Elissa Rabellino**
Proofreaders: **Desne Ahlers, Virginia McLean, Renée Myers, Gail Nelson-Bonebrake**
Contributing Editor: **Laura Buller**
Indexer: **Ken DellaPenta**

Creative Director: **Gaye Allen**
Photographer: **Chris Shorten**
Business Manager: **Richard Van Oosterhout**
Art Directors: **Angela Williams, Emma Forge**
Production Director: **Chris Hemesath**
Production Designers: **Janis Reed, Lorna Strutt, Leon Yu, Joan Olson**
Design Consultants: **Mark Paulson, Crystal Guertin**
Illustrator: **Matt Graif**
Photographer's Assistant: **Mona Long**

SPECIAL NOTE ON SAFETY PRECAUTIONS

At Gymboree, we encourage parents to become active play partners with their children. As you enjoy the enriching activities described in *Baby Play* with your baby, please be sure to make safety your priority. While the risk of injury during any of these activities is low, Gymboree encourages you to take every precaution to make sure your child is as safe as possible.

To reduce the risk of injury, please follow these guidelines: Do not leave your baby unattended, even for a brief moment, during any of the activities described in this book; be particularly cautious when participating in the activities involving water because of the risk of drowning; ensure that your baby does not place in his or her mouth any small objects (even those depicted in the photos) as some may pose a choking hazard and could be fatal if ingested; make sure crayons, markers, and other writing materials are nontoxic and approved for use by children under three years of age.

Throughout *Baby Play* we have suggested guidelines to the age appropriateness of each activity, but please assess your own baby's suitability for a particular activity beforehand, as ability, balance, and dexterity vary considerably from child to child.

While we have made every effort to ensure that the information in this book is both accurate and reliable and that the suggested activities are both safe and workable when an adult is properly supervising, we disclaim all liability for any unintended, unforeseen, or improper application of the recommendations and suggestions featured in *Baby Play*.

PLEASE NOTE

To avoid showing a preference for either gender, use of the words "he" and "his" is alternated with "she" and "her" throughout this book and generally corresponds to the gender of the baby shown in any accompanying photograph.

CONTENTS

FROM BIRTH
0
AND UP

3
MONTHS
AND UP

6
MONTHS
AND UP

CONTENTS

9 MONTHS AND UP

TYPES OF ACTIVITIES

continued ▶

TYPES OF ACTIVITIES

FOREWORD

DR. WENDY S. MASI AND DR. RONI COHEN LEIDERMAN

THE ARRIVAL OF YOUR BABY is a time of celebration and wonder. Your infant appears so tiny and fragile but is actually an incredibly capable and complex individual. At birth she can see, hear, smell, and respond to touch. In fact, for several months she has been hearing while inside the womb and can already recognize your voice. From the very first moment your baby lovingly gazes into your eyes, turns to listen to your voice, or snuggles against your chest, she is letting you know how much she wants and needs your love and attention.

We have spent the last thirty years researching infancy and child development, playing with babies, and talking with their parents—and we have loved every minute of it. Between us, we have raised six children, making us keenly aware of the challenges and the incredible joy and pride being a parent brings into your life. We have learned most parents want the same thing for their children: a happy and fulfilling life. And we have learned there are many paths that lead to that goal.

We firmly believe in the power of nurturing, positive relationships and a playful approach to parenting. Our belief is reconfirmed daily by new scientific research demonstrating that brain development is strongly influenced by the kinds of early experiences our children receive. Your newborn's brain is only 25 percent developed, but by the time your child is three, more than 90 percent of her brain development will be complete.

To achieve her greatest potential, your baby needs you to provide a variety of interesting learning experiences.

Gymboree, America's foremost provider of parent-and-child play programs, developed its "play with a purpose" philosophy to teach parents that the most important way for young children to learn is through play. Through active, hands-on play, your child will learn language, develop problem-solving skills, and master social relationships. Of course parents benefit from play, too. What can compare to the elation we experience when our baby reaches out for us, giggles and dances to her favorite tunes, or mimics us and claps her hands together for the first time?

With this book, Gymboree Play and Music Programs have created a wonderful resource for parents, a compilation of activities and songs to inspire you to interact with your baby on a whole new level. The interchanges you share will support your baby's physical, emotional, and cognitive development and—most important—will help establish a loving, joyful connection. You are your baby's first and most important teacher, treasured companion, and playmate. Rejoice in her discoveries and celebrate each remarkable achievement. Have fun with your baby and enjoy these incredible years. You are getting your baby off to a great start!

Wendy Masi
Dr. Wendy S. Masi

Roni Leiderman
Dr. Roni Cohen Leiderman

MORE THAN FUN

WHEN YOU FIRST BRING a new baby home, your thoughts are usually full of practical matters: how to keep your baby clean, warm, and well-fed; where to store the tiny diapers and clothes; how the front pack, car seat, and stroller actually work; and when you can get some sleep!

You need to concentrate on such logistics, of course; they're crucial for the survival of this wee creature. But once the necessities are taken care of, there's something further that even the littlest baby needs in order to thrive: warm, playful interactions with the caretakers around him.

Dozens of studies in recent years have shown that a child's sense of self-esteem and his ability to form close emotional ties with others greatly depend upon the quality of his bond with his parents. This bond can be greatly enhanced by close, loving play. Indeed, for babies who cannot yet go to school, read a book, or watch a documentary on television, play is the primary way they learn.

THE INCREDIBLE FIRST YEAR

During their first year of life, babies undergo a profound mental, physical, and social awakening. They learn to recognize their families, the closet that holds the crackers, and the playground with the big twisty slide. They learn to support their heads, use their hands, roll over, sit, crawl, stand, and—in some cases—walk. And long before they are ready to speak, they learn to understand a whole range of human communication, from body language (the head shake that discourages further food throwing, for instance, or the open arms that encourage a hug) to some of the words that flow from

LEARNING is only part of the fun.

FROM BIRTH AND UP

FROM BIRTH AND UP
0

AT FIRST GLANCE, your newborn may seem unable to do much. He can't see across the room, hold up his tiny head, or recognize your face.

Indeed, most newborns hardly seem aware of who or what is around them. But appearances are deceiving. The miniature human you hold in your arms is actually taking in volumes of information about his world through all his senses. Though he can't see things more than fifteen inches away and may not recognize your face at first, he definitely knows your smell, your touch, and the sound of your voice (a baby's ability to hear, smell, touch, and taste are fully developed at birth).

In these early months he will also make steady gains in his ability to control his muscles. Sometime in his second month his tightly closed fists may begin to open; if you place a light rattle or other toy in his palm, he'll close his fingers around it. Soon after that he'll try to swipe at objects—perhaps at your dangling necklace or the bunny printed on his blanket. That swipe may be accidental the first time, but soon it will become purposeful—a sign of the beginning of his ability to use his hands to bring objects into his world. His social

skills are developing rapidly, too. He'll gaze intently at you when you speak to him in these early months. In response to different stimuli he'll perfect a range of cries that will bring you to his side. By the time he's six weeks old, he'll add cooing, gurgling, and smiling.

Play during this early period isn't so much about lively activity as it is about sensory exploration—bringing objects to your baby for him to watch, listen to, and touch. Early play also consists of activities that help you and your baby tune in to each other. These can be comforting activities like singing and rocking, or more interactive games like making funny faces for him to imitate or helping him do baby-sized sit-ups. Such responsive interactions are wonderful for developing a loving, intimate bond.

But equally important is learning when to let your baby simply be. Newborns can't yet regulate the amount of stimulation flooding their nervous systems, and they can't tell you when they've had enough. Clues that your baby is getting overstimulated include crying, turning or looking away, and closing his eyes. Respecting your baby's unique needs will help him feel understood and cared for—which is important for his sense of trust.

19

3 MONTHS AND UP

3 MONTHS 3 AND UP

BY THE RIPE OLD AGE of three months, your baby is no longer a newborn. She can hold her head up and turn it toward you when she hears your voice. She can wave her fists and kick her feet when she gets excited.

She may even have mastered that charming whole-body shake that is a baby's way of expressing sheer joy. And she can grin, giggle, grimace, coo, gurgle—and of course cry—to express either pleasure or displeasure.

The second three months of your baby's life introduce the dawn of her sense of control over her world, however elementary. No longer a passive newborn, your baby is stronger and more active and can now use her hands to reach out and pull objects into her world and then turn them, drop them, shake them, or put them in her mouth as a means of exploration. Such activities aren't just a source of entertainment for your baby. They're also learning experiences through which she develops all kinds of essential skills along with her sense of self.

As a parent, you may also be feeling more in control. Your baby is probably sleeping a little longer at night, which means you're getting more sleep, too. You're more familiar with her moods, expressions, and

sounds, so you feel more confident about your ability to take care of her. And as you see that the things you offer—a playful "hello" or an exuberant smile—make her smile, then chortle with delight, you feel more adept at being a parent and at this mysterious activity we call play.

Your baby may also be sitting up, rocking when she's lying down, or even rolling all the way over. This brings up important questions of safety. Your baby won't give you advance warning of her burgeoning mobility, so you never know when she may roll off the changing table or across the floor or wiggle her way under the couch.

This time also ushers in a whole new era for play. Now that your baby is a little stronger, she'll enjoy songs with basic hand and body movements, toys that shake and rattle, and activities such as knee and ankle rides and active tickle games that require her to use her whole body.

The reward of playing with your baby in these early months is the wonder of interaction—being able to see how much she enjoys it. With a rich (and ever increasing) repertoire of vocalizations, she will express her heartfelt enjoyment of tickles, songs, silly faces, brightly colored toys, and—most endearing—the sight of your beloved face.

LEARNING to crawl creates opportunity for more adventurous play activities.

a parent's mouth. At the same time, they learn to communicate their own needs and feelings through their own baby language.

But the greatest task in the first year is the development of a baby's trust. Your baby needs to know that his physical needs for food and warmth will be fulfilled; that his environment is safe; and, most important, that his caretakers will cherish him and nourish his own budding feelings of love. Hugging, kissing, rocking, and smiling are all ways of cultivating this trust. So is introducing the joys of all kinds of play.

Interacting with your child is vitally important throughout his life, of course. But in the first year play can be especially important and rewarding. Researchers estimate that 50 percent of a human's

brain development occurs in the first six months of life; 70 percent is complete by the end of the first year. While much of this development has to do with genetic heritage, a good portion of a child's later intellectual, emotional, and physical life depends upon the kinds and amount of stimulation she receives in her earliest years.

Such talk of stimulation and mental development can sound awfully dry, as though parents should be putting their babies through drills to achieve certain objectives by certain ages. But play comes naturally to most babies—and to most parents, although they may feel intimidated by a

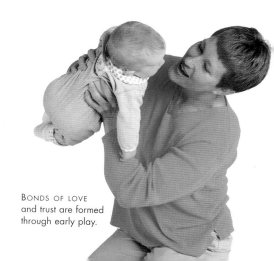

BONDS OF LOVE and trust are formed through early play.

newborn or daunted by their eleven-month-old's lust for life. You can inspire yourself by remembering babies aren't born knowing how much fun the world can be, and you get to show them.

ALL KINDS OF PLAY

Babies don't know that stuffed animals are for hugging or that peekaboo games provide riotous good fun, that pouring water from one cup to another is challenging, or that pinwheels sparkle as they spin. Bringing these games and toys to your baby, along with your attention, laughter, and encouragement, lets both of you share in the explorations. It also teaches your

GAMES that inspire smiles and giggles can also help build happy memories.

baby that she has entered a world that is fun, interesting, and responsive.

Another task for parents during this first year is to tune in to their babies as individuals. Play, even "stimulating" play, isn't really about force-feeding experiences, but is rather about understanding your baby's temperament: her likes and dislikes and her tolerance for and ability to adapt to stimulation. Some babies love to be rocked back and forth in a parent's arms; others strongly object. Some babies like to be chased around the house; others are terrified of such rowdy behavior. Playing works best when it is in response to a baby's cues and follows her lead.

A GENTLE KISS provides the perfect end to a knee ride.

6 MONTHS AND UP

6 MONTHS AND UP

THE SIX- TO NINE-MONTH-OLD BABY is a charmingly social creature, one who laughs, calls out, and smiles to garner attention or provoke a response.

In most cases, he's also a mobile baby, one who can creep, crawl, roll over, scoot, or pull himself up to get what he wants. And at this age, he is truly starting to know and attempting to get what he wants, whether it's the pretzels on the table, the picture book on the shelf, or the stack of plastic bowls in that distant closet. You could call it the budding of baby will. In fact, it signals the development of his ability to recognize an intention (I want that doggie's tail), make a plan (I'll crawl over and grab it), and carry it out (I got it!).

This ability to make and carry out a plan is crucial for what specialists in child development call self-efficacy—the sense that a person has some control over his actions and his world. For many parents, their baby's ability to make decisions is a reassuring signal that he is beginning to understand and interact with his world.

His emerging fine motor skills also continue to engage him. You may find him fiddling with labels or crumbs, carefully bringing his thumb and forefinger together,

or stroking your hair. Most babies at this age also dive into endless emptying—and occasional filling—games. One morning he may take all the cereal out of his bowl, for instance, and then carefully put it back piece by piece, or he may pull all the bibs out of the bottom drawer and then try to stuff them back in.

Around six months is also the age at which your baby begins to grasp the concept of object permanence—the idea that an object exists even when it isn't immediately visible. Now he may look for the object he drops rather than just forgetting about it once it's out of his sight, or he may actively search for a favorite toy in his basket. Such conceptual developments make peekaboo and other hiding games possible. You may get the first glimpses of your baby's own sense of humor when he pulls a towel over his face and then shakes with glee as you pretend to look for him.

Social games of any sort are sure to delight your six- to nine-month-old because he's so much more aware of his relationships with others now. Whether you're playfully calling his name from behind him, mimicking his exclamations of "imi!," "abba!," and "goo!," or blowing raspberries on his belly, he'll see your good-humored interactions as more evidence that the world is a fun and loving place.

23

9 MONTHS AND UP

9 MONTHS AND UP

THE NINE- TO TWELVE-MONTH-OLD PERIOD could rightly be called the "pre-toddler" age. By their first birthdays, even those babies who aren't yet walking are beginning to look and act like toddlers. The rapid growth of baby-hood slows, babies' faces often get leaner, and their ability to assert themselves, move, and communicate gets stronger and stronger.

Games that allow your baby to practice gross motor skills—crawling, pulling himself up to stand, toddling across the floor, or climbing—are particularly appealing to him now, because mobility is his main objective. Fine motor skills are equally important to him. He may insist on turning the pages of a book, for instance, or stacking up a pile of his own books. For many babies, this is the beginning of the "do it myself" stage. He can't say those words yet, of course, but he may be struggling to master activities that a few months ago seemed far beyond his reach.

That's one reason why pre-toddlers enjoy imitative play so much. Your baby now takes an interest in and would like to do what grown-ups do. He'll also experiment with cause and effect, manipulating toys with knobs, spinning dials, and levers that make toys pop up.

A tot-sized tool (a push mower, a cooking set, or a car)

gives him a chance to indulge in such play, which eventually (usually around age two) evolves into games of "pretend," an early form of symbolic thinking. Tot-sized toys also cut down on frustration. It's far easier to manage a tiny pan than a full-sized one, and successfully manipulating toys gives your baby the pride of accomplishment that builds a secure sense of self-esteem.

Some children may use a few words at this age—words like "baba," "mommy," and "duck." More children, though, have their own language consisting of exclamations ("ah jah!," "doo-ick!," "oooooh!") and gestures (pointing, head shaking, reaching both hands toward an object). They'll understand the association between your words and gestures, too—a shaking head means "no"; clapping and cheers constitute praise.

These kinds of associations make finger plays and other song games particularly enticing at this age. While he may not yet be able to master the pat-a-cake words or motions, your baby will still enjoy the rhythmic sounds and simple movements of the game—and your performance of them. It won't be long before he'll be putting on a show for you instead.

SILLY GAMES are terrific at mealtime, too.

a soothing dance. Play "I'm gonna get you!" as you're leaving the house together and you'll get out the door quicker—and probably in better humor. Burst into song in the car and your baby's fussing may turn into giggles. Viewed this way, play becomes less about achieving accomplishments and more about creating relationships. When you play with your baby, you're engaging in intimate activities that help him master certain skills while also creating a loving, long-lasting, and joyful bond.

Babies have distinct cycles of rest and activity, attention and inattention. The best time for active play—swatting at toys, rolling balls, singing songs, or practicing climbing—is when your baby is alert and receptive. More passive play—watching tree shadows, listening to songs, or snuggling up with a book—is easier when he is a little less alert. Both types of play are important. It's the timing that counts.

Spontaneity can make play even more fun and rewarding, and you'll find opportunities at every turn. Add peekaboo games to a diaper change and you may help reduce your child's squirming and wriggling. Tuck your baby in a sling as you mop the floor and household chores become

CHANGING TIME is playtime when you add peekaboo.

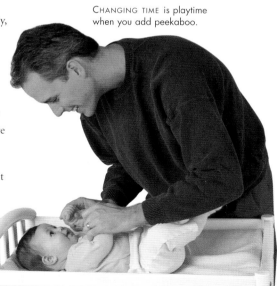

PLAY ACTIVITIES

THE FOLLOWING PAGES contain more than one hundred activities, all designed to engage and stimulate babies throughout their first year and to make the most of the time you spend playing together. You'll find suggestions for every type of meaningful play, from making funny faces and introducing peekaboo, to playing in the bathtub and singing silly songs, so you can choose the activities that best suit your child's mood and interests. All of these loosely structured, open-ended activities can be enjoyed with a minimum amount of equipment and a maximum amount of loving interaction. So flip through these pages, see what new experience you and your baby are ready for, and let the play begin!

A GUIDE TO ACTIVITIES

I **F YOU'RE LIKE MOST** parents, you're probably long on love but short on time. To help out, *Baby Play* offers a number of quick-reference features so busy parents can learn about playtime activities at a glance. These features ensure that each activity is easy to find, simple to understand, and quick to implement, allowing you to spend less time reading directions and more time enjoying worthwhile activities with your child.

Song lyrics, chants, and rhymes appear on a yellow background and frequently include suggested hand and body motions.

Cross-references point to related activities your baby might also enjoy because they are similar in topic or spirit.

Research Reports highlight recent scientific findings that reveal how babies develop and learn during their first year.

Each activity includes concise, easy-to-follow instructions as well as information on how to vary activities and, where appropriate, how to adapt them to appeal to your baby as he grows.

Age labels show the recommended optimal starting age for each activity. This book is divided into four age ranges. (For details on the developmental stages associated with each age, see the Introduction on page 18.) The labels provide a broad guide to help you find an appropriate activity for your baby, but most activities can be adapted successfully for babies from birth to twelve months of age.

BUBBLES FOR BABY

REACHING, TOUCHING, POPPING

SKILLSPOTLIGHT

Watching bubbles float through the air helps your baby practice his visual skills such as eye tracking and distance and depth perception. Trying to swat at them is excellent practice for his budding eye-hand coordination. And if he catches one, he'll get a lesson in the relationship between cause (I touch the bubble) and effect (The bubble pops!).

Cause and Effect	✓
Eye-Hand Coordination	✓
Visual Development	✓

MAKING YOUR OWN

For the soap solution, mix 1 cup of water, 2 tablespoons of glycerin (available in pharmacies), and 2 tablespoons of dishwashing detergent. Make bubble wands from plastic lids with the center cut out. But be sure to keep these away from your baby.

H AS IT BEEN DECADES since you last pondered the magic of bubbles floating in the air? Don't let that stop you from sharing this simple—and highly entertaining—activity with your baby.

• Use a variety of bubble-blowing toys, and blow different-sized bubbles for your baby. If you aim large bubbles at a cloth, soft carpet, or bath water, the bubbles will stick longer, which will give five- and six-month-olds a chance to "catch" their first one. Or create a shower of small bubbles by blowing quickly through a wand or pipe. Tracking bubbles in similar hones an infant's developing visual skills.

• A cascade of bubbles makes a pleasant distraction during diaper-changing time. Blowing bubbles while he's bathing will make bath time fun too (the bathtub also helps contain the soapy residue that some bubbles leave on surfaces). Bubbles following outside are especially enchanting. Try waving the wand way up high in the air, or blow the bubbles low to the ground so they drift skyward on air currents.

BUBBLES ARE FASCINATING BAUBLES— even for very young babies.

132

Skill Spotlights explain the developmental focus of each activity and also contain a quick-reference checklist of its benefits.

Making Your Own provides suggestions on how to fashion makeshift toys and props from inexpensive, everyday materials.

Color photographs of babies— often pictured with a parent or an older sibling—demonstrate each activity in the book.

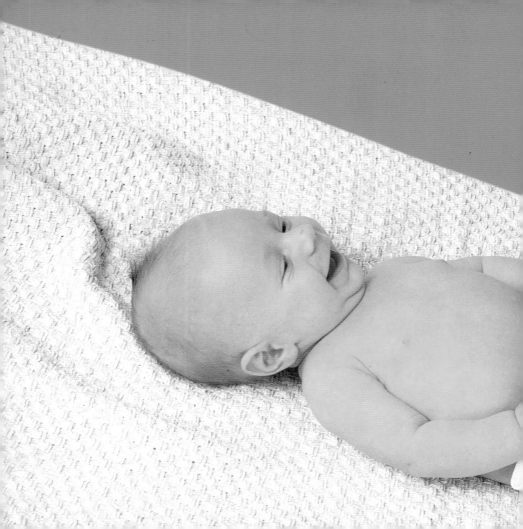

FROM BIRTH AND UP

0

SWAYING, SWAYING

SKILL SPOTLIGHT

The sensory stimulation provided by this activity—the sound of your voice, the feel of your hands, and the sight of your face—can reassure and soothe your baby. This activity may even put her to sleep. And as she approaches three months, your smiles and words may inspire her to coo and grin socially in return.

Body Awareness	✔
Listening	✔
Visual Development	✔

S HE LOVES TO HEAR your voice, she loves to feel your touch, and she loves to be rocked rhythmically from side to side. You can combine all three of these soothing elements by using your lap as a cradle and your voice as a lullaby. Sit in a chair with your baby lying on your thighs and her feet pointing toward your stomach. Cradle her head with your hands and gently sway your body from side to side as you talk or sing to her.

If your baby enjoys this activity, also try **Blanket Swing,** page 64. ▶

GAZING INTO HER EYES as you sway from side to side—that's what builds the deepest ties.

FROM BIRTH
0
AND UP

33

POM-POM PLAY

SKILLSPOTLIGHT

Watching a brightly colored object move from side to side and up and down helps strengthen your baby's eye muscles so that he can track objects and focus at different distances, a skill that requires "visual convergence," or having the two eyes working together. Feeling the pom-poms gently touch his torso, face, and limbs lets him explore new textures.

Tactile Stimulation	✔
Visual Development	✔
Visual Tracking	✔

BABIES AREN'T BORN knowing how to visually track an object or how objects move through space. Such developments take time. This gentle activity will engage your baby's attention, stimulate his senses, and eventually make him smile.

• Gather together some large brightly colored pom-poms or small plush (that is, stuffed) toys. Get your baby's attention by holding the toy twelve to fifteen inches above his face. Slowly move the toy from side to side, matching your pace to his ability to track the object with his eyes.

• Try slowly lifting the object up and down so he can watch it moving from near to far. Touch the toy to his torso, or use it to stroke his face and arms. Of course, you shouldn't leave the baby unattended with small objects.

A TINY YELLOW POM-POM is intriguing to a baby, especially when it brushes his skin.

INFANT MASSAGE

SKILLSPOTLIGHT

Touch is deeply reassuring for infants, especially if it's done calmly and gently. A mild massage stimulates your baby's circulation, sense of touch, and awareness of her body. Look at and talk to your baby during the massage to strengthen your all-important emotional bond.

Body Awareness	✔
Emotional Development	✔
Social Development	✔
Tactile Stimulation	✔

CULTURES AROUND THE WORLD have practiced various forms of infant massage for thousands of years. You can take a class or read books on this topic, but it's also easy to start with very simple forms of massage at home with your baby. Find a warm room or a sunny spot on the bed or carpet. Take off all her clothes except her diaper—or massage her naked on a thick towel or other cloth. If you like, you can use a vegetable-based oil, such as almond or apricot, but be sure to avoid baby oil and other petroleum-based products.

• Using a milking motion, gently squeeze down each arm and leg. Then move your hands from the center of her torso out to the sides. Or softly brush your fingertips over her skin. Speak or sing to her at the same time.

• Place your fingers on her temples and make very small, gentle circles. Then place your fingertips in the middle of her forehead and draw them slowly along her eyebrows. Try gently moving your thumbs along the bridge of her nose, down around her nostrils, and to the corners of her mouth.

SHE LOVES TO FEEL YOUR TOUCH, see your eyes, and hear your voice.

"Touch," writes Theresa Caplain in the classic *The First Twelve Months of Life,* "is almost a language for infants." Indeed, numerous studies have shown that touching your baby—holding her, kissing her, and stroking her—helps deepen bonding. It can also help her physiologically. Research shows that babies who are touched have increased immune functions, improved muscle development, and greater production of growth hormones.

FROM BIRTH
0
AND UP

CRYING AND COLIC

YOUR BABY'S CRY will become as familiar to you as the shapes of his toes. That won't make dealing with it any easier. Some days you'll feel nothing but sympathy; other days your patience will be pushed to its limits.

Babies cry in response to unpleasant experiences, including pain, hunger, loneliness, fatigue, or being chilled or overheated. Some researchers also believe that at three to six weeks, some babies start crying in the early evening simply to let off steam after a long day.

A "colicky" baby cries more persistently and more often than others. Researchers don't know what causes colic. Some have said that colicky babies may have immature digestive systems, or that they may just have a harder time dealing with the world's stimuli. Whatever the cause, even the most loving parents can feel inadequate, anxious, or even angry when faced with the nonstop, shrill cries of a colicky baby.

Some people may tell you to let your baby "cry it out." Most pediatricians these days would disagree.

Comforting your baby—or at least trying to comfort him—shows him that he can count on you to respond to his needs and that distress eventually ends.

What you can do for your baby: If burping, changing, or feeding your baby doesn't help, try motion (such as walking with the baby in a stroller or front pack, or rocking, dancing, or swinging). Fresh air can quiet a crying baby. And young babies often appreciate being swaddled.

What you can do for yourself: Try to catch up on missed sleep. Fatigue makes parents more vulnerable to depression and short tempers, which can make it hard to respond wholeheartedly to your baby's cries. Ask someone to watch the baby while you take a shower or go for a walk. Don't feel you're abandoning your baby. Think of it as replenishing your diminished resources. ■

DANCE WITH MY BABY

SKILLSPOTLIGHT

While the movement may be familiar to him, being held closely in your arms is still a new—and delightful—experience. Listening to the music stimulates his sense of hearing. Feeling you sway and step stimulates his budding sense of balance. And dancing together gazing into each other's eyes is great for social and emotional development.

Emotional Development ✔
Listening ✔
Rhythm Exploration ✔
Social Development ✔

HE ROCKED AND SWAYED in the womb for nine long months, and his life on the outside should be just as filled with stimulating movement. Dancing with a young baby is a wonderful way to calm him and make him feel loved. Holding your baby securely against your chest, dance slowly and smoothly around the room to any kind of rhythmic music: classical, country, gospel, even rock and roll (although not too loud). The dance movements replicate the movements he felt when he was in the womb and also stimulate his sense of balance.

If your baby enjoys this activity, also try **Swaying, Swaying,** page 32.

YEARS FROM NOW, you and your son may both remember the songs that used to soothe him.

41

FACIAL EXPRESSIONS

SKILL SPOTLIGHT

You may have noticed that your baby began scanning your face—or moving his eyes from your hairline to your chin—almost as soon as he was born. That's evidence that faces are very, very important to young babies. Having time in which he can simply look at your face and its expressions lets him begin to make important attachments and learn social cues for affection.

Emotional Development	✔
Listening	✔
Social Development	✔
Visual Development	✔

NOT ALL THE ACTIVITIES you do with your baby have to be vigorous—or even active. Quiet time is equally important. Babies, especially newborns, are easily overstimulated. And intimacy between parent and child depends as much on touch and eye contact as it does on giggles, tickles, and toys. In other words, time spent simply gazing into your baby's eyes is time well spent, as it allows the two of you a chance to relax and bond.

• Choose a time when your infant is alert and receptive. Cradle him in your arms, prop him up on your knees, or lay him down on the changing table or a soft blanket on the floor.

• When he's looking at you, gaze into his eyes. Speak or sing his name softly. Introduce him to some facial expressions: an opened mouth, raised eyebrows, a stuck-out tongue. Then go back to simply looking at him and saying his name softly.

• Your baby may surprise you by imitating your expressions; even the littlest babies will sometimes mirror the face of a caregiver. But if he grows restless or turns away repeatedly, stop the activity. Babies need to withdraw from intense interactions to process all they've experienced.

42

RESEARCHREPORT

Parents' faces and sounds don't just entertain a baby; they can actually make him feel more secure. A University of Delaware study found that the infants of mothers with more animated facial expressions were more securely attached to their mothers than the infants of mothers with less animated expressions. And numerous studies of depressed or withdrawn mothers have found that their infants also tend to be less attached and expressive.

LOOKING TIME is bonding time when it's gentle and responsive.

43

LULLABIES

T'S HARD TO SAY why simple melodies soothe infants, but generation upon generation of parents have sung songs to their little ones, and generation upon generation of little ones have thus been lulled. Lots of lullabies just seem to beg babies to fall asleep, but any quiet song, sung lovingly, can induce sleep, or at least settle an overstimulated baby.

CRADLE SONG

 to the *tune* of **Brahms' Lullaby**

Lullaby, and good night—
go to sleep little baby.
Close your eyes now
sweetly rest.
May your slumbers be blessed.
Close your eyes now
sweetly rest.
May your slumbers be blessed.

WHETHER IT COMES from an older sibling or a parent, a tender song is a time-honored way of calming infants.

HUSH, LITTLE BABY

Hush, little baby, don't say a word,
Papa's gonna buy you a mockingbird.

And if that mockingbird won't sing,
Papa's gonna buy you a diamond ring.

If that diamond ring turns brass,
Papa's gonna buy you a looking glass.

If that looking glass gets broke,
Papa's gonna buy you a billy goat.

If that billy goat don't pull,
Papa's gonna buy you a cart and bull.

If that cart and bull turn over,
Papa's gonna buy you a dog named
Rover.

If that dog named Rover don't bark,
Papa's gonna buy you a horse
and cart.

If that horse and cart fall down,
you'll still be the sweetest little
baby in town.

ALL THE PRETTY HORSES

Hush a bye, don't you cry,
go to sleepy little baby.

When you wake, you shall have
all the pretty little horses.

Blacks and bays, dapples and grays,
all the pretty little horses.

Hush a bye, don't you cry,
go to sleepy little baby.

SINGING A SONG to put your
baby to sleep is soothing to
both you and your infant.

HANKIE WAVE

SKILLSPOTLIGHT

Watching the cloth wave back and forth at this age will boost your baby's ability to visually track and focus on objects. But by three months, she won't be able to resist reaching out and trying to grab the cloth. And by six months, she'll be gumming the cloth as soon as she gets it into her tiny grasp.

Listening ✔

Visual Stimulation ✔

NE OF THE BEST-KEPT SECRETS about playing with young babies is that you don't always need fancy toys with electronic bells and whistles. In fact, sometimes just a cloth handkerchief or colorful scarf will do. Place your baby on her back on the floor or changing table. Hold a scarf, handkerchief, or lightweight cloth about twelve inches over her head. Bring the fabric close to her, then lift it farther away, and bring it down again. Call her name or sing gently to her as you wave the cloth.

If your baby enjoys this activity, also try **Rippling Ribbons,** page 68.

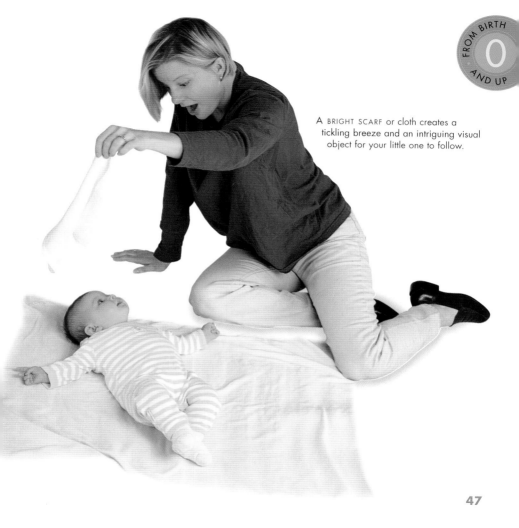

A BRIGHT SCARF or cloth creates a tickling breeze and an intriguing visual object for your little one to follow.

PLAY TIME, WORK TIME

SKILLSPOTLIGHT

After spending nine months in your womb, a very young baby can find it disconcerting if you're not nearby. Keeping your baby close to you throughout the day gives him the security that he needs to develop trust, a key element of his social and emotional growth. And as your baby gets older, he'll love watching you go about your day-to-day routine and will even want to play along.

Emotional Development ✔

Social Development ✔

Y OU CAN'T PLAY with your baby during every one of his waking hours. You both need some downtime. But he'll love to be snuggled close to you as you take care of the usual household chores, such as sweeping, doing the dishes, folding laundry, going grocery shopping, even raking leaves and planting flowers. Just put him in a secure front pack, make sure he's comfortable, and start your routine. Singing and talking to him will soothe him; the rhythm of your movement may lull him to sleep. And you'll no doubt be pleased to get some things done!

If your baby enjoys this activity, also try **Swaying, Swaying,** page 32.

48

Sweep, sweep...sleep, sleep: He'll be lulled by the sound of your voice and your rhythmic movements.

49

LINE ART

SKILL SPOTLIGHT

Putting up interesting objects or pictures of faces provides visual stimulation. But these objects are generally stationary and don't invite all-important interaction. Having you standing by, moving and talking about the objects, both captures your baby's attention more readily and provides a chance for the two of you to interact. In a few short months, she'll be batting at the objects with her hands and feet and delighting in making them dance.

Eye-Hand Coordination	✔
Spatial Awareness	✔
Visual Stimulation	✔

WITH HER NEAR VISION working well but her distance vision still blurry, a newborn is most attuned to objects and movements within a close range. You can purchase an activity gym, or you can create your own appealing visual arrangement for her with some objects found around the house.

• Securely thread a half dozen large plastic binder clips or clothespins onto a length of rope or thick cord.

• Hang pictures, cloth balls, rattles, bows, or small plush toys from the clips, and then be sure to tie the cord securely across the crib or above the changing table.

• Move the toys gently and talk to her about each one. Watch as your baby gazes at each bright toy.

• When her attention wanes or if she fusses or keeps turning her head away, take the rope or cord down. You can play again some other time. Just be sure the cord doesn't fall into the crib, and never leave a baby unattended with the cord.

THESE TEMPTING TOYS are close enough for her to focus on—and far enough away to safely entice her when she begins to reach out.

BABY SIT-UPS

SKILLSPOTLIGHT

All babies learn to hold their own heads up, of course, but gentle exercises like this one strengthen the torso and upper-body muscles. They also give your baby a taste of the wonders of the world still to come. Once your baby can control his own head, he can decide what he wants to look at and for how long.

Balance	✔
Body Awareness	✔
Upper-Body Strength	✔

A NEWBORN'S HEAD is very large and heavy compared with his small body. That heaviness, combined with the fact that his neck muscles are so weak, means that he can hold up his own head only briefly. You can help him sit up and strengthen his muscles by guiding him through this simple game. Lay your baby down on a blanket on his back. Using the blanket as a sling, grasp the edges with both hands close to the top of his head. Pull him up gently, then lower him again. Repeat several times.

If your baby enjoys this activity, also try **Blanket Swing,** page 64.

YOUR BABY WILL LOVE looking at you, and he gets a gentle workout to boot!

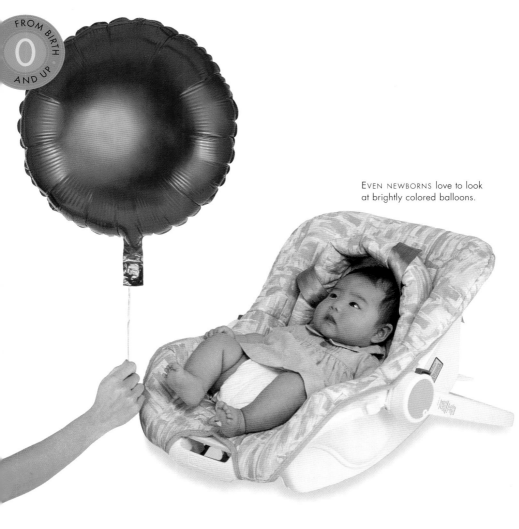

FROM BIRTH
0
AND UP

EVEN NEWBORNS love to look at brightly colored balloons.

BOUNCING BALLOONS

 A **BABY'S ABILITY** to see far away isn't well developed in her early months, but that doesn't mean she's not intrigued with the visual world. Give her something fun to look at by holding a Mylar balloon or two so that she can see them. (Babies should never be left alone with balloons or their strings.) Then watch your baby's eyes widen with wonder as the balloons bob in the breeze! You can try blowing on the balloons and tugging their strings, too, to make their movements more dramatic.

SKILLSPOTLIGHT

Watching the bobbing balloons helps your baby develop both visual focus and visual tracking skills. By talking to your baby and tugging the balloons, you make this game interactive, which reinforces your relationship, too.

If your baby enjoys this activity, also try **Rippling Ribbons,** page 68.

✔ **Social Development**

✔ **Visual Development**

A MIRROR PROVIDES a fun-filled play experience for the whole family.

WHO IS THAT?

NEWBORNS ARE MORE ATTUNED to real human faces than to any other visual object, including rattles, geometric shapes, or even drawings of human faces. In her earliest weeks, a baby stares at faces even though she doesn't know that they, like her, are human. That means she'll be fascinated by her own tiny reflection in a handheld mirror—even though she'll have no idea who it is. Hold a mirror up so your baby can see her reflection. Point at the baby in the mirror, and say her name. As she grows older her reflection will prompt that first sign of sociability—the infant's impish grin.

If your baby enjoys this activity, also try **Facial Expressions,** page 42.

SKILLSPOTLIGHT

A baby won't recognize herself in the mirror until she's around fifteen months old. But even in her earliest months, gazing at herself in the mirror helps her learn to visually focus and track as well as to explore the social nature of faces. Eventually, it will help her identify herself as both a baby and a unique being.

✔	**Emotional Development**
✔	**Social Development**
✔	**Visual Development**

AIRPLANE BABY

SKILL SPOTLIGHT

Parents around the world have spent many long hours comforting colicky babies by swinging them gently back and forth in an "airplane" hold. The steady pressure along the baby's tummy provides soothing warmth and tactile input. And with every passing week she'll practice lifting her head, neck, and shoulders so that she can widen her baby's-eye view.

YOU MAY HAVE ALREADY DISCOVERED that a classic "airplane" or "football" hold calms your baby when she's gassy, overwhelmed, or just tired. Combining a swinging or swaying motion and a rhythmic song with that firm hold around her belly can be even more calming. Just support your baby, tummy down, by holding her under her chest and belly with one or both of your arms. (But always be sure to support a newborn's head.) Then swing her gently to and fro while singing a rhythmic song.

Tactile Stimulation	✔
Trust	✔
Upper-Body Strength	✔

If your baby enjoys this activity, also try **Dance With My Baby,** page 40.

WITH A LITTLE BIT OF WIND
in her little bit of hair and with
Mommy's arm supporting her,
she's soaring like a glider.

59

TICKLE-ME TEXTURES

SKILL SPOTLIGHT

Your baby's skin is about as sensitive to touch now as it ever will be, and touch is one of a baby's primary ways of exploring the world. This tactile activity introduces your child to a wide range of textures. It also gives you an opportunity to practice recognizing and responding to her body language. Such attuned responses help build her sense of security as she witnesses that someone is taking care of her needs.

Body Awareness	✔
Social Development	✔
Tactile Stimulation	✔

NEWBORNS DON'T ALWAYS LIKE to be undressed because the air feels cold on their skin. Older babies frequently fuss during diaper changes because they don't want to be restrained. You can turn changing time into play and learning time by providing your baby with interesting tactile experiences.

• Gather several objects with different textures. Try swatches of fabrics such as velvet and corduroy, feathers, or a clean sponge dampened with warm water.

• Gently rub an object across your baby's skin and watch for her response. Try a different object. Look for clues such as smiles that indicate her preferences.

• This is an activity that can entertain your baby for many months. Sometime after her ninth month, she may find the texture toys and hold them out for you to tickle her with!

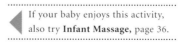

If your baby enjoys this activity, also try **Infant Massage,** page 36.

THE FEATHERY TEXTURE makes
her squirm with delight.

CRADLE SONGS

Y **OUR BABY** won't actually giggle at a tickle until he's about three months old. Tactile games will intrigue him, however, and will boost his budding awareness of his own body. And incorporating silly songs or chants will appeal to his innate fascination with the human voice.

DID YOU EVER SEE A LASSIE?

Did you ever see a lassie,
a lassie, a lassie,
did you ever see a lassie
go this way and that?
walk your fingers slowly back and forth
across baby's body

Go this way and that way,
go this way and that way,
did you ever see a lassie
go this way and that?
walk your fingers slowly back and forth
across baby's body

YOUR TOUCH and the sound of your voice are all he needs to have fun.

YANKEE DOODLE

**Yankee Doodle went to town
a-riding on a pony;
stuck a feather in his cap
and called it macaroni.**

**Yankee Doodle keep it up,
Yankee Doodle dandy;
mind the music and the step
and with the girls be handy.**

TWINKLE, TWINKLE LITTLE STAR

Twinkle, twinkle little star,
hold hands up, opening and closing fists
how I wonder what you are!

Up above the world so high,
point upward
like a diamond in the sky.
*create a diamond with thumbs
and forefingers*

Twinkle, twinkle little star,
open and close fists
how I wonder what you are!

LITTLE PETER RABBIT

 to the *tune* of "John Brown's Body"

**Little Peter Rabbit had a fly
upon his nose.**
touch baby's nose

**Little Peter Rabbit had a fly
upon his nose.**
touch baby's nose

**Little Peter Rabbit had a fly
upon his nose.**
touch baby's nose

And he flipped it, and he flopped it
"shoo" fly near baby's face

till it flew away.
make flying motion

HEARING A SIMPLE SONG
while in Daddy's arms
is always a delight.

BLANKET SWING

SKILL SPOTLIGHT

The rocking motion provided by this simple swing can soothe your baby. It will also help her learn about balance—something she needs for learning to sit up—as her body shifts from side to side in response to the momentum. If she tries to lift her head off the blanket, she'll strengthen her neck muscles. And having two loving faces smiling down at her reinforces her feelings of trust.

Balance	✔
Social Development	✔
Trust	✔
Upper-Body Strength	✔

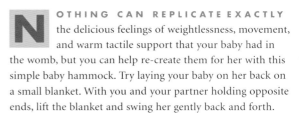

NOTHING CAN REPLICATE EXACTLY the delicious feelings of weightlessness, movement, and warm tactile support that your baby had in the womb, but you can help re-create them for her with this simple baby hammock. Try laying your baby on her back on a small blanket. With you and your partner holding opposite ends, lift the blanket and swing her gently back and forth.

Change the movement sensation for her by slowly lifting the blanket up and down. You can also lift one end of the blanket to raise her head slightly and lower her legs, to help her sit up and look around. But it's the motion, eye contact, and singing that make this a fun activity for everyone.

If your baby enjoys this activity, also try **Dance With My Baby,** page 40.

Sway, Sway

to the *tune* of **"Hey, Ho, Nobody Home"**

Sway, sway, sway, sway,
now reach up and
touch the sky.
Then fall gently
like the snow
down to the ground.

THIS SIMPLE SWING is as relaxing for
a baby as a hammock is for adults, and
it also teaches her about balance and trust.

GETTING ORGANIZED

WHEN YOUR BABY is born, your home is filled with the presence of a precious new being. It also gets filled with a whole lot of baby "stuff." It's not just the crib, stroller, and changing table you bought before the baby's due date. Your home will also be bursting with everything from tiny clothes and diapers to bottles and assorted toys.

Having a perfectly tidy house isn't the top priority of most new parents. But adapting your expectations and household organizing systems should be. Remember that you can't get as much done as you did in pre-baby days. Be flexible. Make lists, but don't berate yourself for not completing every task.

At your fingertips: Diapers, diaper wipes, rash ointment, and clothing should be kept within arm's reach of the changing table so you don't leave the baby unattended. And baby washcloths, soaps, and towels should be close by at bath time.

Like with like: You can use baskets or plastic boxes to keep toys sorted.

Keeping clothes organized by size and season—all of the things that fit now in the top drawer, and all of the things that are too big but might fit in the summer in another—also helps. Having a system makes it easier for you—and any other caretakers—to find the right clothes quickly.

For a rainy, or later, day: You don't have to put out every toy, book, and article of clothing you receive. Toys meant for an eighteen-month-old can be stored; you'll be glad to have some new toys when the time comes. Older-baby clothing can be sorted and tucked away in a closet.

Tidy up: You can't expect to have all the household chores done all the time. But you can decide to do one job once a day. Whether you do it in the evening, or during the baby's afternoon nap, making the house somewhat neat can be a balm for a parent's soul. ■

FROM BIRTH · 0 · AND UP

SHE'S NOT QUITE OLD ENOUGH to reach out and grasp yet, but she still loves the movement.

RIPPLING RIBBONS

LONG BEFORE YOUR BABY is eagerly tearing paper off packages, ribbons will capture her curiosity and attention. Using masking tape, attach six-inch lengths of brightly colored ribbon to a piece of cardboard, or tie them securely to a wooden spoon. Lay your baby on the floor or changing table, or in an infant car seat. Gently wave the ribbons around her face and hands. When she starts kicking her feet and jerking her arms, you'll know she's having fun with the colors, textures, and movement.

SKILL SPOTLIGHT

At this age, watching the ribbons dance from side to side and up and down helps your baby develop her visual tracking skills. When she is older and starts swiping at objects, this activity lets her practice her eye-hand coordination and grasping skills, and lets her see the relationship between cause (I hit the ribbon) and effect (the ribbon swings and bounces).

✔ **Eye-Hand Coordination**

✔ **Tactile Stimulation**

✔ **Visual Development**

If your baby enjoys this activity, also try **Dance With My Baby,** page 40.

SOUND SPOTS

SKILL SPOTLIGHT

Listening and looking for your voice helps your baby develop both his visual tracking and auditory location skills. Equally important is your introduction of the idea that his family provides smiles, laughter, and praise. By the time he's six months old, he, too, will be smiling and laughing, and by the time he's one year old, he'll be trying to get you to turn your head toward him when he makes funny sounds.

Listening	✔
Social Development	✔
Visual Development	✔

BABIES ARE BORN with an innate fascination with human voices, but they're not born with an immediate ability to locate the source of a sound in a room. To help your baby fine-tune his senses, try this: Place him in a car seat or infant chair in the middle of a room. Walk back and forth in front of him as you sing songs, make funny noises, or talk to him. Then try walking to the opposite side of the room and back again, letting him follow the sound of your voice. Although he won't turn his head at the sound of your voice, he'll hear the difference in sound as you move back and forth.

If your baby enjoys this activity, also try **Noisemakers,** page 78.

FROM BIRTH
0
AND UP

Most parents get a kick out of claiming that their infant's personality—be it calm, restless, sweet, or belligerent—was foretold by his activity in the womb. But do such links between prenatal behavior and postnatal personality have any merit? In fact, researchers at Johns Hopkins University have found that several factors, including movement in the womb and heart rate, really can help predict what an infant's temperament will be during his first few months. According to the study, more active fetuses generally turn into livelier and more unpredictable infants.

FINDING MOMMY'S VOICE
will eventually evolve into
fun games of peekaboo
and hide-and-go-seek.

EYES ON TRACK

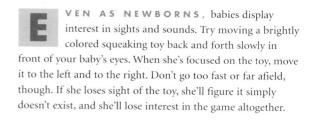

SPOT THE TOY

What's that sound? What's that movement? As your baby moves her head from side to side, she learns to locate the source of noises and keep track of an object's whereabouts. At around three months, she'll swipe at the toy, and at about four months, she'll start to grab at it.

E VEN AS NEWBORNS, babies display interest in sights and sounds. Try moving a brightly colored squeaking toy back and forth slowly in front of your baby's eyes. When she's focused on the toy, move it to the left and to the right. Don't go too fast or far afield, though. If she loses sight of the toy, she'll figure it simply doesn't exist, and she'll lose interest in the game altogether.

Listening ✔

Visual Tracking ✔

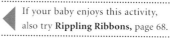

If your baby enjoys this activity, also try **Rippling Ribbons,** page 68.

SHE'S VERY INTERESTED in a
toy's sound and movement,
even if she's not old enough
to reach out and grab it yet.

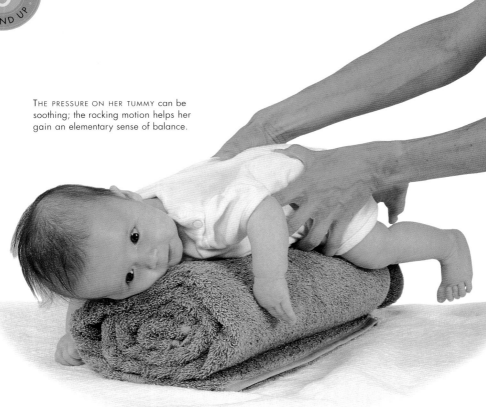

THE PRESSURE ON HER TUMMY can be soothing; the rocking motion helps her gain an elementary sense of balance.

ROCK THE BABY

BALANCE ON A BOLSTER

WHEN WE THINK OF ROCKING, we usually think of a baby on her back in a cradle or in our arms in a rocking chair. But another very soothing motion for an infant is to be gently rocked from side to side on her tummy. Roll up a towel or two together. Lay your baby on her stomach over the roll so that it supports her head, chest, stomach, and thighs. Turn her head to one side. Then very gently rock her from side to side while singing a song such as "Rock the Baby" (see the lyrics at left). The rocking motion helps her develop a sense of balance, while lying on her tummy gives her a chance to try to lift her head from a belly-down position.

If your baby enjoys this activity, also try **Beach-Ball Balance,** page 76.

Rock the Baby

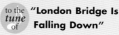
to the *tune* of "**London Bridge Is Falling Down**"

Rock the baby
side to side,
side to side,
side to side.
Rock the baby
side to side,
just like this.

✔ **Balance**

✔ **Spatial Awareness**

✔ **Upper-Body Strength**

BEACH-BALL BALANCE

A ROCK AND ROLL GAME

SKILLSPOTLIGHT

Rolling back and forth and from side to side stimulates a baby's sense of balance. After the first month, most babies will also try to lift up their heads to see what's going on around them. That motion helps build upper-body strength. And the gentle pressure on the tummy can help babies with gas or colic.

Balance	✔
Trust	✔
Upper-Body Strength	✔

YOUNG BABIES often don't like to lie on their tummies for very long. But most find it pretty interesting to lie on something big, soft, and round for a little while. Try placing your baby tummy-down on a slightly deflated beach ball. Then, while securely holding her, rock her slowly forward and back or side to side on the ball. (But always be sure to support a newborn's head.) Sing or talk to her while you play; that will help keep her focused while the gentle rhythm and pressure soothe her tummy. Stop when she gets tired.

When she's older and nearly able to sit up on her own, you can support her seated on top of the beach ball, and very gently bounce her up and down.

If your baby enjoys this activity, also try **Rock the Baby,** page 74.

BRIGHT COLORS, a squishy surface, and a delightful rolling sensation make a winning combination.

NOISEMAKERS

SKILL SPOTLIGHT

Hearing the various sounds from the dangling objects will sharpen your baby's auditory awareness and his visual discrimination skills. Seeing the objects will help him focus. And in a few months, when your baby is able to swipe at objects, this activity can encourage him to develop his gross motor skills.

Eye-Hand Coordination	✔
Listening	✔
Visual Development	✔

WHETHER THE SOUND is familiar, such as music from a favorite mobile, or unfamiliar, like a new voice, noises intrigue even the youngest babies. Create a primitive symphony of sound by stringing a number of noisemaking objects—jar lids, lightweight rattles, or plastic and wooden spoons—on a rope or ribbon. Dangle and shake the noisemaker about twelve inches in front of your baby. Or string it across the crib and let him gaze up at it as you shake the rope or jiggle the objects for him—just don't leave him alone with this kind of toy.

If your baby enjoys this activity, also try **Sound Spots,** page 70.

RATTLES, TINKLES, and jingles will grab your baby's attention and help him learn how to locate the source of sounds.

79

LITTLE BIRD-WATCHERS

BABY'S FIRST NATURE CLASS

SKILL SPOTLIGHT

A newborn will have trouble seeing the birds clearly, but she may detect a blur of color or motion. Over the next few months, watching birds will help her develop her visual tracking and focusing abilities. Her curiosity about the birds is a great example of her blossoming fascination with the world around her. A year from now—believe it or not—she'll be begging to help you fill the feeder!

| Listening | ✔ |
| Visual Development | ✔ |

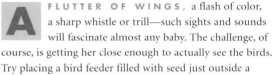

A FLUTTER OF WINGS, a flash of color, a sharp whistle or trill—such sights and sounds will fascinate almost any baby. The challenge, of course, is getting her close enough to actually see the birds. Try placing a bird feeder filled with seed just outside a window. As the birds begin to flock, hold your baby up so she can see them, or place her infant seat where she can watch them come and go. Soon she'll be crowing delightedly when she sees her feathered friends.

If your baby enjoys this activity, also try **Bubbles for Baby,** page 132.

SHE LOVES TO WATCH these
funny, flying creatures flit about.

81

BABYCYCLE

SKILLSPOTLIGHT

By moving his legs for him, you let your baby feel his little legs and feet moving in a new way— each side of the body working in reciprocal movement. You also mimic an action he'll be using later on as he learns to crawl.

| Body Awareness | ✔ |
| Gross Motor Skills | ✔ |

WHEN HE'S FIRST BORN, your baby has no idea that his body is actually separate from yours. But his expanding physical abilities will give rise to an increased interest in his own body parts that will last him well into toddlerhood. They also let him enjoy more physical, interactive games. In this simple exercise game, you very gently and very slowly move his legs in a bicycling motion, all the while talking and smiling at him to encourage him to wiggle his legs without your help. Before you know it, he'll be grabbing his own little feet— and eventually pedaling all by himself!

If your baby enjoys this activity, also try **Infant Massage,** page 36.

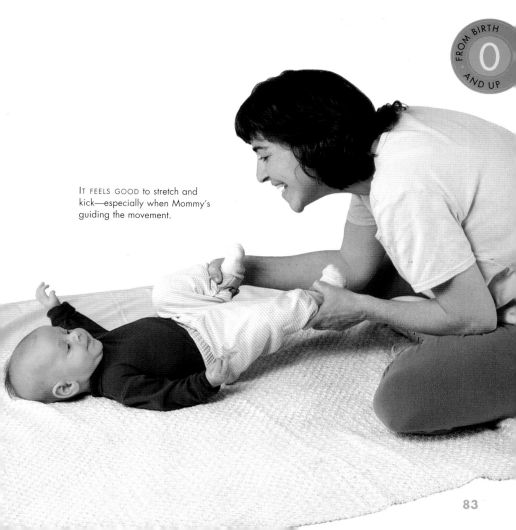

IT FEELS GOOD to stretch and kick—especially when Mommy's guiding the movement.

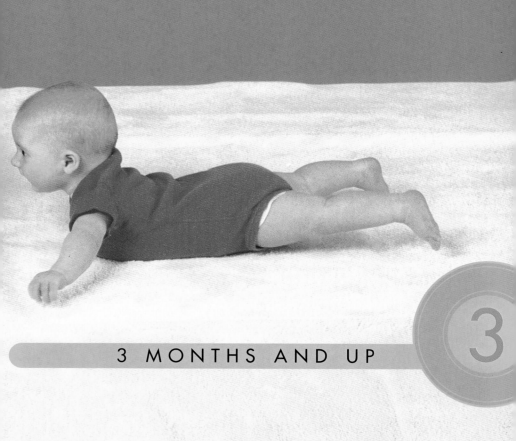

3 MONTHS AND UP

3

STRETCHING OUT

I'm a Tiny Baby

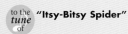 **"Itsy-Bitsy Spider"**

I'm a tiny baby
I'm soft and round and small.
But when I'm busy stretching
I feel so big and tall.
My arms are getting long,
and my legs are getting strong.
And the next thing you know,
I'll be learning how to crawl.

*See page 105 for the lyrics of
"Itsy-Bitsy Spider."*

Body Awareness ✔
Tactile Stimulation ✔

AFTER NINE MONTHS in the womb, a newborn often arrives with a tendency to continually curl up in, yes, the fetal position. Gentle stretching exercises can help him become aware of his tiny arms and legs. Lay your baby down on his back on a bed, a changing table, or the floor. Very gently stretch his arms up over his head and then down again. Try bringing one of his arms up while drawing the other down along his body. Then bring one arm up while carefully stretching the opposite leg down.

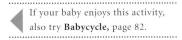
If your baby enjoys this activity,
also try **Babycycle,** page 82.

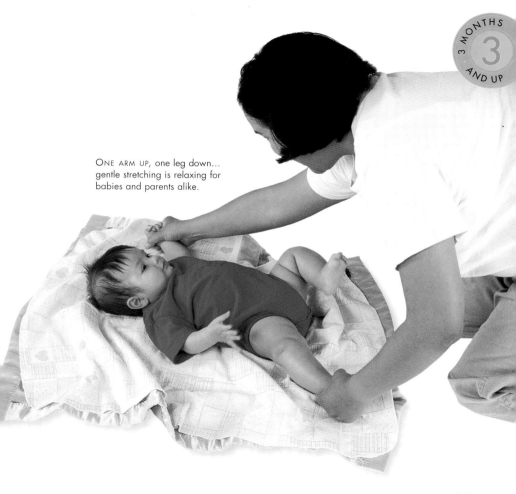

ONE ARM UP, one leg down... gentle stretching is relaxing for babies and parents alike.

WHEN YOUR BABY is grasping a pink plush puppy, she is exercising her ability to reach out and make contact with her world.

SWAT THE TOY

YOUR BABY may be able to see (at close range) as well as you can, but her ability to grasp objects is still not a match for yours. To help her, attach a small plush toy or teething ring to a brightly colored ribbon or chain of plastic links. Dangle the toy in front of her and make it sway from side to side, encouraging her to reach across her body. Praise her efforts as she reaches out and swipes at—or even grabs—the toy. But never leave a baby alone with a long ribbon, as it poses a safety hazard.

SKILL SPOTLIGHT

By three months, most babies are using their heads and eyes together to track moving objects. That is, if an object moves to the left, the baby rotates her head to the left to follow the object, rather than just moving her eyes, as a newborn does. But she still needs to practice her grasping skills. Reaching for a moving object helps her fine-tune the coordination of both sides of her body.

✔ **Eye-Hand Coordination**

✔ **Fine Motor Skills**

✔ **Visual Development**

If your baby enjoys this activity, also try **Big Bouncing Ball**, page 134.

ROLL ME OVER

SKILLSPOTLIGHT

Learning how to roll over is usually preceded by several weeks of rocking from side to side. It's generally not until a baby is about five months old that she is strong and coordinated enough to go from back to stomach or stomach to back. This activity helps your baby practice using both sides of her body, which is required for this basic movement.

Balance	✔
Bilateral Coordination	✔
Body Awareness	✔
Gross Motor Skills	✔

BABIES AREN'T BORN knowing how to roll over, although it may seem they are, from the way they rock and squirm around on the changing table at this age. They actually learn how to roll at around five or six months of age. Give your baby a head start toward mastering this important milestone and developing bilateral coordination by helping her roll from her stomach or back up onto one side. Place her on her stomach or back on one side of a towel or blanket and gently lift it a bit, so she rolls onto her side. Or gently push her back and forth so she learns how to swing her weight correctly. You may need to help her lift her arm out of the way as she starts to roll.

If your baby enjoys this activity, also try **Tick-Tock,** page 114.

90

A GENTLE TUG on the blanket gets her moving in the right direction.

TARGET PRACTICE

SKILLSPOTLIGHT

For babies, eye-foot coordination is important. Eventually, using his feet in conjunction with his eyes will help your baby cruise the furniture and learn to walk.

Body Awareness	✔
Eye-Foot Coordination	✔
Listening	✔

HE'S ALREADY DISCOVERED the joy of kicking his little legs. Give your baby's kicking a purpose by holding a target for him to try to hit. When he's on his back—on the changing table, a bed, or the floor—hold up a pillow, a soft toy, your hands, or a pie tin within easy reach of his little feet. If he doesn't understand the game, guide his feet to the target and praise him when he makes contact. Once he figures out what to do, he'll want to practice this one over and over.

HE SEES HIS FOOT make contact, he hears the resulting noise, and he feels the sole of his foot on the plate.

PEEKABOO GAMES

SKILL SPOTLIGHT

A newborn baby thinks that when an object disappears, it no longer exists. When you appear and disappear behind the diaper, she begins to learn that even if you're momentarily hidden, you're still there. Grasping this concept—that is, holding mental images—is a precursor to language development. When she gets old enough to put a blanket over her own face (albeit haphazardly), you'll see her kick and squirm with joy, as she's now in control of the disappearing act.

| Object Permanence | ✔ |
| Social Development | ✔ |

FIRST MOMMY'S THERE, then Mommy's gone, and then she's back again. Peekaboo is a perennial favorite with babies. Sometime around six or seven months, babies start to understand that objects continue to exist even when they are not present. Peekaboo is a great way to explore this concept with your little one. You can hold a blanket or diaper in front of your face while you say "Where's Mommy? Where's Mommy?" and then peek out from behind. Or put a light towel over your baby's face instead, then whisk it off, calling, "Peekaboo!" when her face emerges.

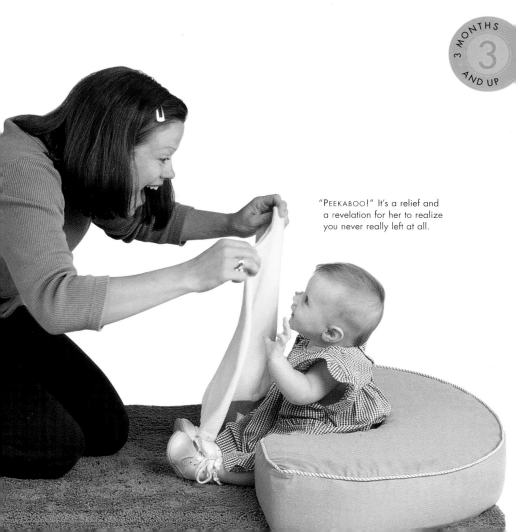

"PEEKABOO!" It's a relief and a revelation for her to realize you never really left at all.

BABBLING WITH BABY

THE LITTLEST LANGUAGE LESSONS

SKILLSPOTLIGHT

Responding to your baby's babbling supports his early efforts to communicate using sounds other than crying. Positive reinforcement of his vocalizations will show him that people value what he has to say, which will make mastering language more rewarding for him in the long run.

Language Development	✔
Listening	✔
Social Development	✔

A THREE- TO SIX-MONTH-OLD BABY is frequently a delightfully social little being full of funny coos, gurgles, shouts, grunts, and irresistible smiles. Although he can't say real words yet (that skill won't come until he's nearing his first birthday), he utters those adorable sounds as a way of exploring the sounds he hears every day. He also learns from the responses you give to these vocalizations. Encourage his early efforts at communication by holding a baby-babble conversation with him.

• When he says "aaah," listen, nod, and say "aaah" in return. When he says, "goo!" you say "goo!" too.

• Once you're both warmed up, try changing his words slightly, by stretching them out ("bah!" becomes "baaaaaaah") or even adding to them ("ooh" becomes "oooh-wah!").

• Encouraging your baby to mimic you will inspire him to try ever more complex language patterns, which eventually will result in his attempting words and then phrases.

Note: This kind of baby talk is constructive only until your child begins talking. At that point, it's better for you to repeat words correctly than to repeat his incorrect pronunciations, no matter how cute they are.

RESEARCHREPORT

For the first six months, babies will babble whether you talk to them or not. But they'll learn how to talk more easily if you make a concerted effort to show them how language works. Indeed, all babies—no matter what language is spoken in their home—sound alike until they're about six months old. After that, they start repeating the sounds they hear most often.

HE'LL SQUEAL AND SQUIRM with delight when he realizes you're following his lead in this elementary conversation.

97

SLEEPING THROUGH THE NIGHT

BY THE TIME she's three or four months old, your baby will probably have developed some sort of sleep pattern. It may be a dream-come-true sleep pattern, or it may feel like your biggest life challenge—waking every hour on the hour at night, never napping for more than half an hour during the day, suddenly getting daytime (wake time) and nighttime (sleep time) reversed, or something in between.

Getting a baby to sleep on a "normal" schedule is actually a matter of common sense and logistics, with a little bravery and patience thrown in.

Develop a daytime routine: plan fairly regular times for outings, baths, play periods, and meals. External regularity will help her set her inner clock.

Develop a nighttime routine: a warm bath, cozy pajamas, a lullaby, and some books are classic ways of getting your baby to unwind. It's never too early to convince a baby that nighttime feedings are all business and kind of boring.

Keep the lights low, don't talk to her very much, don't let her play with toys or watch television, and gently put her in her crib on her back as soon as she's done.

Once your baby is about six months old, she shouldn't really need to eat during the night. If a baby fusses once in bed, some parents choose to use a modified "cry it out" program, letting her cry for a few minutes, then going in to reassure her, then letting her cry some more. Some continue to feed, cuddle, walk, or sing to their baby in hopes that eventually the child will sleep longer and longer on her own. Eventually, most babies will learn to put themselves to sleep, which is an important skill to have.

What's the best approach for getting a baby to sleep through the night? It's a little bit different for every family. The magic formula is the method that you and your baby feel most comfortable with—and that's a personal decision. ■

TUMMY BOLSTER

SKILL SPOTLIGHT

Using a bolster like this one helps your baby practice putting weight on his forearms, which helps him strengthen his arm and back muscles in preparation for sitting up and eventually crawling. And giving him a new position from which to view the world will stimulate his vision and inspire him to reach, roll, or even creep forward.

| Social Development | ✔ |
| Upper-Body Strength | ✔ |

LEARNING HOW TO SIT requires far more than just keeping one's head up; it also calls on the muscles of the shoulders, torso, and upper and lower back. You can help your baby develop those muscles by bolstering him with a soft "pillow." Roll up a towel, securing the ends with soft fabric hair bands, and then slip the towel roll under his arms and chest while he lies on his tummy on the floor or carpet. The bolster helps him to raise his neck and shoulders up for longer periods and encourages him to use his arms for support. This position also offers him an enticing view of the world around him.

If your baby enjoys this activity, also try **Tummy Talk,** page 108.

HE'LL GET A NEW PERSPECTIVE on his world when he's perched up on his chest this way.

101

FRIENDLY FACES

SKILLSPOTLIGHT

The combination of your baby's visual abilities and desire for human interaction makes her highly sensitive to cues provided by facial expressions. A book full of different faces gives her many to contemplate. She may simply stare at them—glancing from their eyes to their mouths and back again. Or she may try to point or talk to the pictures.

MAKING YOUR OWN

You can create a face book by gluing photos (either from magazines or from your own collection) on pieces of heavy cardboard. Preserve them with clear plastic contact paper or sheet protectors. Or simply place photos in a photo album.

BY THE AGE OF THREE MONTHS, your baby is so attuned to facial expressions that she responds to smiles or laughter. She can also tell the difference between her loved ones' faces and unfamiliar faces. That's why you get that special grin when your baby peers at you over someone else's shoulder and your friends just get a solemn gaze. It's also why her whole body wriggles when you peek at her over her crib rail in the morning; she recognizes your face, and she already loves it dearly. Giving your baby a book with lots of faces—either one you buy or one you make—introduces your baby to a wide range of faces and the many emotions they express. You may even find that she develops favorites—perhaps the little boy gleefully holding a puppy, or the picture of Daddy looking sheepish in his fishing hat.

Social Development ✓

Visual Discrimination ✓

POINTING OUT THE PEOPLE in your family photos helps your baby begin to connect names with familiar faces.

RHYME TIME

L **ULLABIES SOOTHE** a fussy baby, but nursery rhymes and other fun songs are important, too. They teach your baby that lilting language and vocal variations can be elements of affection and play. They're often easy to remember, too, because the lines rhyme.

BAA BAA BLACK SHEEP

Baa baa black sheep,
have you any wool?
Yes sir, yes sir,
three bags full.
One for the master,
and one for the dame,
and one for the little boy
who lives down the lane.

A-HUNTING WE WILL GO

Oh a-hunting we will go,
a-hunting we will go.
We'll catch a little fox
and put him in a box,
and then we'll let him go.

SEE-SAW, MARGERY DAW

See-saw, Margery Daw,
Jack shall have a new master.
He shall have but a penny a day
because he won't work any faster.

LITTLE JACK HORNER

Little Jack Horner
sat in a corner
eating a pudding and pie.
He put in his thumb
and pulled out a plum
and said, "What a good boy am I."

ITSY-BITSY SPIDER

The itsy-bitsy spider went
up the water spout,
down came the rain and
washed the spider out.

Out came the sun and
dried up all the rain,
and the itsy-bitsy spider
went up the spout again.

PEAS PORRIDGE HOT

Peas porridge hot,
peas porridge cold,
peas porridge in the pot,
nine days old.

Some like it hot,
some like it cold,
some like it in the pot,
nine days old.

NURSERY RHYMES introduce your
baby to the idea that language,
like music, is rhythmic.

MIRROR PLAY

A THREE- OR FOUR-MONTH-OLD BABY is just getting to the point where she can amuse herself for several minutes on end—an exciting breakthrough for baby and parents alike. You may hear her gurgling to her toes early in the morning, for instance; see her fiddling with her hands in front of her face; or catch her looking intently around a room. At around four months old, a baby can not only see but also track, which means that she can actually watch items or people as they move around her. Now that your baby can lift her head while she's on her tummy, a mirror in her crib can provide a lot of fun. She doesn't yet understand that the reflection in the mirror is her, and won't until she is fifteen to eighteen months old. Still, she'll brighten and smile when she sees her own face—she's happy to be greeted by such an intriguing person!

YOUR BABY WILL BE ENCHANTED by her new playmate, even if she doesn't recognize that it is her own image.

SKILL SPOTLIGHT

Watching her own face and interacting with her image in the mirror increases your baby's budding awareness of herself as a separate person. And if she lies on her stomach, it will help her strengthen the muscles needed for sitting and crawling.

✓ **Upper-Body Strength**

✓ **Visual Stimulation**

TUMMY TALK

SKILL SPOTLIGHT

Every moment your baby spends on his tummy helps build up his strength. Your reassuring presence and pride in his accomplishments (however small) also help him learn that it's really OK to be on his stomach. When you roll him back over if he gets too uncomfortable (as indeed you should), your baby learns yet again that someone is paying attention to his cues and responding appropriately.

Emotional Development	✔
Social Development	✔
Upper-Body Strength	✔

AT THREE MONTHS, some babies may still cry in protest when placed on their tummies. But spending time in that position is crucial, as it helps them to strengthen the neck, shoulder, and back muscles in preparation for sitting and crawling.

• You shouldn't make your baby stay in a position he is not comfortable with, but you can persuade him to like it more by lying in front of him, placing a favorite toy in view, making eye contact, and socializing with him a bit.

• Encourage him if he starts to improvise with different body positions. He may start "swimming" excitedly with his arms and legs, for instance. Or he may stiffen them in an "airplane" position and rock back and forth.

• Don't worry if your baby can tolerate being on his belly for only a minute or two. Follow his lead and quit when he has had enough. You can always try again later. Plenty of babies find tummy time challenging—and all of them eventually learn to sit, crawl, and walk.

RESEARCH REPORT

You may be aware of the concern of some doctors that sleeping on the back (currently advised for preventing "crib death" or Sudden Infant Death Syndrome) may slow babies' gross motor skill development because their neck and back muscles don't get as much exercise. In fact, recent research shows that while some back sleepers roll over and crawl later than tummy sleepers, both types learn to walk at about the same age.

IF MOMMY'S DOING IT, then he may decide it's OK for him to try it a while, too.

GETTING OTHERS INVOLVED

IT'S A FACT that in most families, Mommy takes on the lion's share of the care for young babies. Unfortunately, the more Mommy does it, the more she—and everyone else—starts feeling that she's the only one who knows how to do it right. Here are a few suggestions to help others get involved with your baby's care and play.

The other parent: If Mom stays at home and Dad goes to work, research shows that she changes ten times as many diapers as he does, prepares three times as many meals, and spends about eight times as long playing with the baby. If they're both working, statistics show, she's still spending more time with the baby. That can make her feel like she's the expert and him feel that he's all thumbs.

How do you let go? Tell your significant other what he needs to know for safety's sake (for example, the baby can now roll off the bed), and then walk away and let him figure it out. If he secures a diaper too loosely or puts the baby in a position she doesn't like, he'll discover his mistake soon enough.

Grandparents: They may have different or outdated ideas about child rearing, or have forgotten how to take care of a baby. But a grandparent's love is special and something your child shouldn't miss. Explaining what works and is safe for your baby will make everyone feel more comfortable. Let the grandparents know what your baby enjoys, and then let them indulge their love.

Babysitters: Regular babysitters will have a good idea of what toys your baby enjoys, what comforts her, and what trouble she's attracted to. Occasional babysitters need to have that information spelled out. Show all babysitters where you keep extra clothing and the first-aid kit. Leave emergency telephone numbers. Then leave! It's important for parents and babies alike to know that little ones are safe in the care of others. ■

GRANDPA'S COLORFUL PINWHEEL will capture the baby's attention and may prompt a gleeful reaction.

PINWHEEL MAGIC

BY FOUR MONTHS, your baby's vision has developed significantly, he can control his head, and he's starting to reach out to touch things. This means he's ready—and eager—to take in the wonders of the wide world. Try showing him the blur of beautiful colors that results when you blow on a pinwheel. He himself won't be able to blow on it until he's more than a year old, but he may enjoy watching you wave it in the air. (Most babies this age will try to grab at pinwheels. Don't let them, however, as the sharp edges could hurt them and small pieces could be swallowed.) You can also place the pinwheel outside in a planter box and seat the baby near it so that he can watch the multiple colors spin round and round.

If your baby enjoys this activity, also try **Swat the Toy,** page 88.

SKILL SPOTLIGHT

A tantalizing pinwheel will mesmerize most babies. A younger baby—around three months—will be fascinated by the blur of movement and may swipe vaguely at the pinwheel with closed fists. By six months, though, he'll be able to see and reach for the pinwheel. You can also sing a spinning pinwheel song to add to the fun.

✔ **Social Development**

✔ **Visual Development**

113

TICK-TOCK

A CUCKOO GAME

Tick-Tock

Tick-tock, tick-tock,
swing baby from side to side

I'm a little cuckoo clock.
swing her from side to side

Tick-tock, tick-tock,
swing her from side to side

now I'm striking one o'clock.
*lift baby up to the sky gently
just once*

Cuckoo! Cuckoo!
*repeat verses with two and three
o'clock, raising baby up two and
three times, respectively*

ITH A SIMPLE CHANT, some soft swaying, and a gentle lift in the air, this activity is sure to please most babies. Hold your baby under her arms and keep her head upright. You can sit or stand with your baby facing you or facing out into the room. Babies also like to watch each other doing this activity. So if your little one has a little playmate, let them face each other while the parents sing the song. When your baby gets too heavy for you to lift this way, you can turn the game into a lap ride by chanting the words as you rock back and forth and gently bounce your baby on your lap.

Balance	✔
Body Awareness	✔
Listening	✔

If your baby enjoys this activity,
also try **Blanket Swing,** page 64.

SHE HAS NO IDEA what a clock is, but swinging from side to side is delightful just the same.

RESEARCH REPORT

You may think your infant isn't paying attention to music. Yet in fact, numerous studies in recent years have shown that babies can remember a melody and comprehend rhythm, and that music even sets off memories for them. In one study of three-month-old babies, researchers played a song while babies played with mobiles. When the babies heard that same song either one day or seven days later, they started interacting with their mobiles once again.

JUST OUT OF REACH

SKILLSPOTLIGHT

Even before your baby can sit up on his own, he may be starting to roll from one side to the other. That means he's beginning to realize he's a self-propelling creature. Entice him with interesting-looking objects to encourage his emerging mobility. Accompanying the exercise with playful interactions helps build a close relationship between you and your child and sows the seeds for healthy self-esteem.

| Gross Motor Skills | ✔ |
| Social Development | ✔ |

 OU CAN ENCOURAGE your baby's early efforts to grab things and even to move his body by placing attractive objects (brightly colored balls, plush toys, favorite picture books, and, most especially, yourself) just beyond his reach. Encourage him to get to the objects in any way he can, whether by creeping forward on his tummy, rolling over on his side, or just plain s-t-r-e-t-c-h-i-n-g as far as he can go. Don't tease him, though. Instead, build success into the activity. If he starts to get frustrated, simply hand him the toy and then praise his efforts.

116

STRETCHING, ROLLING, and
"tummy time" build strength
needed for crawling.

BELLY ROLL

SKILL SPOTLIGHT

The gentle massage from the beach ball provides tactile stimulation and helps a baby become aware of his own body. Grasping the ball helps him develop eye-hand coordination. When he gets older, sitting upright and holding on to the ball with your support will help him learn balance.

Balance	✔
Body Awareness	✔
Tactile Stimulation	✔

WHEN HE WAS FIRST BORN, your baby couldn't tell the difference between his being and your being, or where his body ended and yours began. You can boost his budding body awareness and stimulate his little body by gently rolling a small inflatable ball across his tummy and up and down his legs and arms. Does he want to grab it or kick it? Let him at it—it's excellent coordination practice. You can also try putting him on his tummy and rolling the ball down his back. Singing a song during this belly-roll activity can add to the fun.

If your baby enjoys this activity, also try **Tickle-Me Textures,** page 60.

THE TICKLING PRESSURE of a rolling beach ball helps him learn more about his body.

KITCHEN FUN

SKILLSPOTLIGHT

As he manipulates cups and spoons by dropping them, picking them up, and placing them in his mouth, your baby learns about using his arms and hands. Exploring objects by mouth helps him learn about physical properties such as smooth, rough, cold, hard, light, and heavy. Your participation in such activities helps ensure your baby's success.

Eye-Hand Coordination	✔
Fine Motor Skills	✔
Gross Motor Skills	✔

JUST BECAUSE YOUR BABY can reach out and grasp something—a rattle, a stuffed animal, or a lock of your hair—doesn't mean he can control that object very well. Becoming truly dexterous requires fine control of the wrist, palm, and fingers, as well as the ability to judge distance and shapes. All that takes plenty of practice. Sets of plastic measuring cups and spoons are great toys at this stage because they're easy to grasp and have interesting surfaces. If your baby has learned to pick up things on his own, just place them around him on the floor. If his aim isn't yet perfected, place the spoons in his hand and encourage him to hold them. Don't be surprised or disappointed if the spoons immediately go in his mouth. Gumming and mouthing objects is a healthy way for babies this age to learn about the world.

EXPLORING WITH SPOONS helps your baby understand how his hands, arms, and various-sized objects actually work.

RESEARCH REPORT

While there is a genetic component to the "handedness" your baby adopts, a mother's style may also have a strong influence. In a study of infant-mother pairs, researchers at DePaul University in Chicago found a baby often matched his mother's handedness (right-handed vs. left-handed) during toy play, and that the matching increased as the baby got older. Sorry, dads—a father's handedness tends not to have as much of an effect, perhaps because statistically moms spend more time with young babies.

121

KNEE RIDES

ADD A LITTLE BOUNCE to lap time by propping up your baby on your knee and gently rocking her back and forth while you sing a children's song. It's a good way for her to gain a sense of rhythm and challenge her sense of balance.

TO MARKET, TO MARKET

To market, to market,
to buy a fat pig,
home again, home again, jiggety jig.

To market, to market,
to buy a fat hog,
home again, home again, jiggety jog.

To market, to market,
to buy a plum bun,
home again, home again,
marketing's done.

TROT, TROT, TROT

Trot, trot to London,
rock baby side to side on lap

trot, trot to Dover.
**Look out (baby's name)
or you might fall O-VER.**
tip baby to one side

Trot, trot to Boston,
rock side to side on lap

trot, trot to Lynn.
*support baby's waist and neck
with your hands*

**Look out (baby's name)
or you might fall IN!**
*gently let the baby drop through
the space between your legs.*

SKIP TO MY LOU

Skip, skip, skip to my Lou,
rock baby rhythmically from side to side
skip, skip, skip to my Lou,
skip, skip, skip to my Lou,
skip to my Lou, my darling.

Lost my partner, what'll I do?
rock baby back and forth
lost my partner, what'll I do?
lost my partner, what'll I do?
Skip to my Lou, my darling.

I'll find another one, prettier too,
raise baby up on knees, and down again
I'll find another one, prettier too,
I'll find another one, prettier too,
skip to my Lou, my darling.

Flies in the buttermilk, shoo fly shoo,
rock baby on knee, exaggerate "shoo" sound
flies in the buttermilk, shoo fly shoo,
flies in the buttermilk, shoo fly shoo,
skip to my Lou, my darling.

MY BONNIE

My Bonnie lies over the ocean,
rock baby to left
my Bonnie lies over the sea,
rock baby to right
my Bonnie lies over the ocean,
lean backward
oh bring back my Bonnie to me.
pull baby tight to chest

Bring back, bring back,
rock baby back and forth
oh bring back my Bonnie
to me, to me.
Bring back, bring back,
rock baby back and forth
oh bring back my Bonnie
to me.
end with
a big hug

FEW BABIES can resist a
silly song and a rhythmic
rock with a parent.

WAY HIGH

SKILL SPOTLIGHT

Although he's firmly held by you, this "flying" activity helps him develop the large muscles in his back and shoulders, especially if he lifts his head up to look at the scenery. It also gives him a chance to develop a fledgling sense of balance. You won't let him go, of course, but he'll feel his center of gravity shifting as he "flies" up and down.

Balance	✔
Upper-Body Strength	✔

YOUR UNCLE HARVEY may have tossed you in the air when you were young—and you may have loved it—but such baby-as-beach-ball activities are no longer considered safe. You can still have fun "flying" with your baby, however—just be sure to keep a steady grip on his tiny torso and keep your movements safely gentle. Sit upright with your baby in front of you on the floor. Lift him up in the air, then roll onto your back, lifting him over your head. You can also place your baby on his tummy on your shins while you lie back and gently sway or lift your legs while holding his arms. Either way, he will enjoy the feeling of soaring through the air, even while you're safely supporting him. Sing a song like "I'm Flying High" (lyrics at right) to add to his fun.

MOMMY'S STEADY HANDS, happy song, and smile make "roughhousing" safe and fun.

I'm Flying High

 to the *tune* of **"Little Teapot"**

I'm a little baby,
I fly high.

Here is the floor,
here is the sky.

Like a little bird
or butterfly.

Now up! I go—
I'm flying high.

BABY'S FIRST BOOKS

SKILL SPOTLIGHT

The physical closeness involved in reading envelops your baby with a sense of intimacy and well-being. Indeed, in time, a reading session can become a wonderful bedtime ritual and a nice way of calming a fretful, sick, or over-stimulated baby. And having the objects in the pictures named for him helps him develop a receptive vocabulary for language.

Emotional Development	✔
Language Development	✔
Visual Development	✔

HE'S TOO YOUNG to understand a story line. He's probably too young even to turn the pages. But introducing your baby to the pleasures of books is one of the best things you can do for him, as it builds a positive association with reading.

• Small, square board books are easiest at this age, as your baby can gum them, hit them, and grab at them without damaging the pages. In the second half of this first year, when your baby learns to turn his own pages, plastic bath books or books with cloth pages will be easier for him to handle.

• Books with colorful pictures and a minimum of text are the best choices, as they introduce him to the magic of illustrated worlds without too much narration. Point out the objects in each picture—"See the duck?" "Where are the socks?" Some-day he'll surprise you by pointing to objects on his own.

• Most young babies don't sit still for a full narration and may enjoy simply exploring the pages, but some babies are lulled by nursery rhymes and story lines. Your baby knows best what kind of storybook session he likes, so follow his lead.

EVEN THE YOUNGEST BABIES enjoy time spent snuggling, listening to words, and looking at colorful pictures.

RESEARCHREPORT

He can hardly sit up and he can't tell a chicken from a dump truck. So why read to a baby? Research shows that reading, even to young babies, helps them build their "receptive" vocabularies (the number of words they understand). In one study at Rhode Island Hospital, researchers compared the receptive vocabularies of two groups of eighteen-month-olds. One group had been read to often as babies, while the other group had not. The frequent-reading group's vocabulary had increased 40 percent since babyhood; the nonreading group's vocabulary had increased just 16 percent.

127

EYES, NOSE, MOUTH, TOES

SKILLSPOTLIGHT

Your baby's not going to repeat any of these body-part names; that comes later on. But your touch provides tactile stimulation for her and helps her become more aware of her body's parameters and movements. Naming body parts often enough eventually will help her to recognize them and learn how to say them herself.

Body Awareness	✔
Language Development	✔
Tactile Stimulation	✔

HER KICKING FEET, waving hands, and general jiggling and giggling are all signs that your baby is beginning to understand that she can somewhat control the movements of her own body. Reinforce this dawning realization by pointing out the major body parts for her. Place her on a bed, carpet, or changing table. Touch her face with your fingers and say "face." Then place her little hands on your face and repeat "face." Then do her eyes, nose, mouth, and chin, and her legs, tummy, feet, and toes, each time letting her feel both her own body and yours.

"THIS IS YOUR FACE, this is my face." Before you know it, she will be touching her own face when you say the word.

FEW BABIES CAN RESIST the sound and sight of a colorful squeaky toy, especially when both parents join in the fun.

WHAT'S SQUEAKING?

BETWEEN THE THIRD and fourth months, most babies learn to reach for and grasp objects. This isn't an easy task; it requires a baby to have significant hand control. It's an exciting discovery, however, as he can now draw objects in the world toward himself, rather than waiting for you to deliver them. To help him practice, hold two squeaky toys in front of him. Squeezing first one and then the other, encourage him to grab at the toys.

SKILL SPOTLIGHT

At first your baby may just wave his hands and kick excitedly. But squeaky toys are enticing enough that he'll start swiping at them—which is good practice for his eye-hand coordination and shows him just how far his body can reach. If he makes contact with the toy, let him hold it; the sense of accomplishment and satisfaction he gets will be a reward that inspires him to try again and again.

| ✔ | Eye-Hand Coordination |
| ✔ | Listening |

If your baby enjoys this activity, also try **Big Bouncing Ball,** page 134. ▶

BUBBLES FOR BABY

REACHING, TOUCHING, POPPING

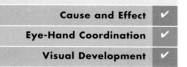

**MAKING
YOUR OWN**

For the soap solution, mix 1 cup of water, 1 tablespoon of glycerin (available in pharmacies), and 2 tablespoons of dishwashing detergent. Make bubble wands from plastic lids with the center cut out. But be sure to keep these away from your baby.

HAS IT BEEN DECADES since you last pondered the magic of bubbles floating in the air? Don't let that stop you from sharing this simple—and highly entertaining—activity with your baby.

• Buy a variety of bubble-blowing toys, and blow different-sized bubbles for your baby. If you aim large bubbles at a cloth, soft carpet, or bath water, the bubbles will stick longer, which will give five- and six-month-olds a chance to "catch" their first one. Or create a shower of small bubbles by blowing quickly through a wand or pipe. Tracking bubbles in midair hones an infant's developing visual skills.

• A cascade of bubbles makes a pleasant distraction during diaper-changing time. Blowing bubbles while he's bathing will make bath time fun (the bathtub also helps contain the soapy residue that some bubbles leave on surfaces). Bubbles billowing outside are especially enchanting. Try waving the wand way up high in the air, or blow the bubbles low to the ground so they drift skyward on air currents.

BUBBLES ARE FASCINATING baubles—
even for very young babies.

BIG BOUNCING BALL

SWATTING PRACTICE

SKILLSPOTLIGHT

He can't grab objects until he can learn to literally aim and fire those little hands and feet. That takes eye-hand and eye-foot coordination, as well as an understanding of just how far those arms and legs extend— all of which comes from steady swatting and kicking practice.

Body Awareness	✓
Eye-Foot Coordination	✓
Eye-Hand Coordination	✓
Visual Development	✓

SOMETIMES IT'S THE SIMPLEST TOYS that give a baby the biggest kick for the longest amount of time. For instance, an old-fashioned, brightly colored punchball (available at toy stores) can engage a baby all through the first half of his first year—and even beyond. Newborns will gaze at the floating orb if it's hung from a ceiling or doorway. Three- to six-month-olds can swat it with their hands, kick it with their feet, and eventually try to get both arms around it. Can't find a punchball? Try hanging a colorful beach ball instead. Whichever you choose, be sure to supervise your baby with the ball.

If your baby enjoys this activity, also try **Pinwheel Magic,** page 112.

134

HE'LL LOVE SWATTING at a big, colorful ball.

JACK-IN-THE-BOX

SKILL SPOTLIGHT

The sound of a crank going round and round, as well as the delicious "pop" of a toy springing from its box, provide auditory stimulation for your baby. Equally important, the repetition of the toy's appearance and disappearance reinforces her growing understanding of object permanence.

Cause and Effect	✔
Listening	✔
Visual Stimulation	✔
Object Permanence	✔

TAKE A GAME OF PEEKABOO, add a little music, throw in the surprise effect of having a toy pop out from a box, and you've got a perfect activity for a five- or six-month-old baby. Once she learns that a toy comes out of the jack-in-the-box every time, the anticipation will build until it's hard for her to contain her excitement. Soon she'll be helping you stuff the toy back in the box, and waiting expectantly for you to close the lid, turn the handle, and make it pop out again.

If your baby enjoys this activity, also try **Peekaboo Games,** page 94.

SHE'LL LOVE having you turn the handle and helping you stuff the clown back in his box.

137

FOOTSIE PRINTS

SKILLSPOTLIGHT

Granted, this activity is as much for the parents (or grandparents, aunts, uncles, or friends) as it is for the baby. But the sentimental value shouldn't overshadow the benefits to him. Feeling the paint and the cloth or paper provides a tactile experience. And participating in a project that requires partnership with a parent and perhaps even another parent-child pair helps his social development.

Social Development	✔
Tactile Stimulation	✔
Trust	✔

IT'S HARD TO BELIEVE your baby's tiny feet will ever be as big as, say, those of the eighteen-month-old next door. But children are always growing. So be sure to capture the memory of your infant's wee size by making colorful footprints.

• Just dab nontoxic paint on his foot (you can use a brush or your fingertip) starting with the toes and moving down to the heel, being careful not to paint the arch. Then stamp his foot, rolling from heel to toes, on to the surface you're working with. You can make prints on a piece of construction paper, some fabric, or a T-shirt, to make a great memento.

• Don't try to make too many adorable footprints in one sitting. When your baby tires, put away the paints for another day.

Note: This activity works best with two adults. You may also want to wear old clothes and keep a box of wipes handy.

PRACTICE MAKES PERFECT with these tiny footprints, but even the mistakes are adorable.

139

6 MONTHS AND UP

6

KICK, KICK, KICK

SKILLSPOTLIGHT

Kicking helps your baby strengthen her leg and abdominal muscles, which is important for crawling and, eventually, walking. With you helping her to lie in the tub, she will develop confidence in the water, which could be helpful later in learning how to swim.

| Gross Motor Skills | ✔ |
| Trust | ✔ |

MOST BABIES TAKE TO BATHS like a duck takes to water, but there are plenty of ways to make bath time even more exciting—and beneficial—for your little one. Six- to nine-month-old babies are often thrilled to be sitting up and splashing in the tub. With the tub filled with lukewarm water and your baby safely seated on a nonslip mat, encourage her to kick, either by praising her natural attempts to do so or by gently kicking her legs for her. You can also hold her so that her belly is in the water and her head and shoulders are lifted safely above the surface. (This position also lets her splash with her arms.) Singing a song like "Kick, Kick, Kick" (see lyrics at right) will encourage her and add to the game's fun.

A LITTLE HELP from you will get your baby kicking and splashing in no time at all.

Kick, Kick, Kick

 to the *tune* of **"Twinkle, Twinkle, Little Star"**

**I am kicking
my little feet.
I am keeping
quite a beat.**

**I am splashing
with my toes.
Look how far
the water goes.**

**I love bath time,
I love kicks.
I love learning
bathtub tricks.**

*See page 63 for the lyrics of
"Twinkle, Twinkle Little Star."*

PUSHING GAME

SKILL SPOTLIGHT

A baby's muscles develop from the head and neck, shoulders, and arms; down the back; and finally to the hips, thighs, and calves. At this age your baby's upper body may be pretty well developed (that's why he can sit up), but his legs aren't quite sturdy enough for him to crawl. This exercise helps strengthen them and also gives him a taste of what it takes to get some forward motion.

Balance	✔
Gross Motor Skills	✔
Upper-Body Strength	✔

HE THINKS HE CAN, he thinks he can…he thinks he can move forward on his tummy, but he's not quite coordinated enough yet. Give him a boost by laying him on his front and letting him push against your hands or a rolled-up towel with his feet. Don't push, but support his feet with your hands as he inches forward each time. One minute of "creeping" practice now and again may be exhilarating; two minutes may be all he needs to get moving down the path toward greater mobility.

If your baby enjoys this activity, also try **Just out of Reach,** page 116.

144

SOMETIMES A LITTLE SUPPORT from behind can help get your budding crawler moving.

6 MONTHS AND UP

SURPRISES INSIDE

HE'S RUMMAGING through the drawers, digging through the magazine rack, and pulling all his books off his shelf.... His constant explorations are probably creating chaos in your home, but they're actually a sign of healthy infant development. Here's a way to put those little hands to good, nondestructive use: loosely wrap some of his toys in brightly colored paper, put them all in a big shopping bag, and let him dig through, unwrap, and rediscover his things. This is a great activity during long car rides, train trips, and airplane rides.

IT'S THE SAME BALL he's had for months, but it's a surprise when he finds it under bright-colored paper.

SKILLSPOTLIGHT

It takes fine motor skills to figure out how to unwrap an object, and your baby will delight in the sound of crumpled paper. You may have to show him how to unwrap objects at first, of course, but once he masters it, he'll soon understand that good things come in wrapped packages.

✔	**Fine Motor Skills**
✔	**Problem Solving**
✔	**Tactile Stimulation**

SHAKE, RATTLE, AND ROLL

SKILLSPOTLIGHT

Mastering the delightful shaking motion and creating the rattling sound will make your baby feel quite powerful and boost his awareness of cause and effect as he replicates the noise over and over again. It will also help him express his growing sense of rhythm and develop his gross motor skills.

MAKING YOUR OWN

Plastic spice bottles work well for homemade maracas because they're small enough for your baby to wrap his hands around. Fill them with sand, dried beans, or pebbles; secure the tops firmly with duct tape or glue; and he's ready to shake!

BY SIX MONTHS, your baby has a pretty good sense that his hands are connected to his arms and has pretty good control of the movements of both his arms and hands. Now he wants to use his hands to explore his environment, whether by patting, stroking, or grabbing at nearly everything around him. As he discovers the properties of the objects he touches—their shape, weight, texture, and, of course, taste—he'll be particularly amazed by the various sounds they make. You can help his early experiments by providing an elementary maraca made from a plastic bottle filled with something that will make noise. Show him how to shake it—but once he gets the idea, it may be hard to get him to stop!

Cause and Effect	✔
Gross Motor Skills	✔
Listening	✔

If your baby enjoys this activity, also try **Music Maker**, page 160.

A BOTTLE FILLED WITH SAND is a simple toy, but the sound it makes is music to your baby's ears.

6

DUMPING OUT TOYS is even more fun with a playmate.

DUMPING DELIGHTS

A PUTTING-IN AND TAKING-OUT GAME

DUMPING THINGS out of containers and then putting them back in again is a favorite sport of babies who have learned to sit up and use their hands. Wherever he is in the house, your baby will probably find something to empty and fill. And while he will be happy to empty out the contents of your wastebaskets or cupboards all morning long, you can let him play a cleaner and more baby-friendly putting-in and taking-out game by giving him a wide-mouthed, gallon-sized plastic jar, a large plastic storage container, or even a large stainless steel bowl of his own. Fill the container with items such as measuring cups, plastic bowls, blocks, and small plush toys. Then sit alongside him and help him fill and dump the container a few times. He will soon be busily doing the job on his own—over and over again.

If your baby enjoys this activity, also try **Baby's Cupboard,** page 188.

SKILL SPOTLIGHT

Besides entertaining your baby, dumping and filling containers teaches him about the relative sizes, shapes, and weights of various objects. It also introduces him to spatial concepts such as big and small, and empty and full. Dumping out items and putting them back exercises both fine and gross motor skills.

✔ **Fine Motor Skills**

✔ **Gross Motor Skills**

✔ **Size and Shape Discrimination**

✔ **Spatial Awareness**

151

BABYPROOFING

WHETHER she's rolling, creeping, crawling, pulling up, or cruising at this stage, a mobile baby is quite capable of harming herself. Some kinds of babyproofing depend on your baby's particular interests (not all babies are fascinated with potted plants, for example.) But some kinds need to be done regardless of your baby's current behavior, because the consequences can be dire.

Electrical outlets: Babies are very curious about tiny holes. Outlet caps and covers are easy to install and can avert a possible disaster.

Cupboards: Any cupboard or drawer that contains sharp, poisonous, or breakable objects needs to have a babyproof lock. Better yet, move dangerous items out of your baby's reach.

Unstable furniture: If your baby bangs into or pulls up on a piece of unstable furniture, she could knock it over and seriously injure herself.

Bolt unstable furniture (such as bookshelves) to a wall and keep heavy objects off furniture that wobbles when touched.

Choking hazards: Keep an eagle eye out for small objects that often fall on the floors of your home, such as needles, coins, pills, or earrings. Regular sweeping and vacuuming can help keep these hazards to a minimum.

Stairs: Install barriers at the top and bottom of each flight of stairs in your home.

Adult stuff: Don't forget to be constantly on the lookout to make sure things like knives, scissors, letter openers, razors, pens, and drink glasses stay out of your baby's reach.

Unfortunately, babyproofing is not a one-step operation. As your baby gets older, taller, more mobile, and bolder, you'll need to monitor what she can hit her head on, what she can reach, and what she can put her fingers into. ■

SWITCHING GAME

SKILL SPOTLIGHT

Passing a toy from one hand to another helps her learn to grasp and release simultaneously—not easy when you're still a baby. It will also help her to cross over the vertical midline of her body with her hands, a necessary precursor to crawling and walking.

Bilateral Coordination	✔
Eye-Hand Coordination	✔
Fine Motor Skills	✔
Grasp and Release	✔

BY NOW YOUR BABY HAS a good grasp of getting hold of objects—whether it's her favorite stuffed elephant or a lock of your hair. But she may not be quite so adept at passing an object from one hand to another, which involves moving two hands at once. (Instead, she'll probably drop one object when offered another.) To help her practice using both hands, put a small toy in one. Let her play with it for a while, then hold another toy up toward that same hand. Encourage her to switch the first toy from one hand to the other, rather than simply dropping it. Her reward for this tricky task? Getting to hold two toys at once!

If your baby enjoys this activity, also try **Dumping Delights,** page 150.

HOLDING TWO TOYS at once takes practice, but the result is twice as nice!

PLAY BALL

SKILLSPOTLIGHT

Having a desirable object move just beyond reach may inspire your baby to pursue the next mobility task, whether it's rolling, creeping, or crawling. Learning how to stop a moving object reinforces her developing sense of personal power as she exerts control over her environment. But don't expect her to roll or throw the ball back to you yet; those are skills she develops in her second year.

Balance	✔
Eye-Hand Coordination	✔
Gross Motor Skills	✔
Spatial Awareness	✔

SHE'S NOT QUITE READY for a game of catch, but a game of fetch will please her no end. Roll a medium-sized whiffle ball or a large plastic or cloth ball just beyond your baby so that she has to move to get it. Or try rolling it to her directly so that she can get used to stopping it with her hands. Hint: Letting a little air out of a ball will make it easier for her to grab and handle.

SHE WILL DELIGHT in stopping a rolling ball—and learning about objects in motion.

RESEARCH REPORT

It's one of those days when you're tired and maybe even a little cross, so you're not quite up to laughing, clapping, and urging your baby on. Can she tell the difference? Studies show that when parents deliberately interact in an emotionally flat way, their babies use facial expressions and vocalizations to try to get them to act "normally" again, evidence that they're seeking to "repair" the interaction. Of course it's OK, and perfectly normal, to have a bad day once in a while. But, if you can respond positively (with a smile and a hug, perhaps), your baby will gain confidence in her ability to regulate social interactions, and it might make you feel better, too.

157

POP! WHEN SHE TOUCHES the bubble, she'll learn more about cause and effect.

BUBBLE

GET THAT BUBBLE

THE THRILL OF THE "POP"

IF YOU'VE ALREADY TRIED BLOWING bubbles for your baby, you know how much little ones enjoy this timeless activity. You may also have noticed that while your baby yearns to reach them, she has a hard time even getting close, which can be frustrating. You can make her goal a little more attainable by catching the bubble on a wand and passing it right in front of her. She'll first get to watch the bubbles float through the air, then get an up-close view of a single shimmering orb. Finally, she'll experience the joy of actually touching it—if only for a moment—and popping it. Be careful that she doesn't rub her eyes with her soapy hands. When you're finished with this activity, wipe her hands with a clean washcloth.

If your baby enjoys this activity, also try **Bubbles for Baby**, page 132.

SKILL SPOTLIGHT

In addition to gratifying her urge to get her hands on those mysterious bubbles, this game lets your baby practice her eye-hand coordination. It also bolsters her understanding of cause and effect and shows her that she can exercise some control over her world.

✔ **Cause and Effect**

✔ **Eye-Hand Coordination**

MUSIC MAKER

Matching an external beat isn't a part of her musical skill set yet, but showing her that music is participatory and fun helps her musical and social development. This activity works on her gross and fine motor skills and sets up a positive association with music.

Fine Motor Skills	✔
Gross Motor Skills	✔
Listening	✔
Rhythm Exploration	✔

IT'S NEVER TOO EARLY to expose your baby to music, but it's not until she's old enough to control objects (even somewhat) that she can become an active player. You can enhance her listening pleasure by giving her things to shake, rattle, and roll while she listens to recorded music or your own singing voice. Just gather together rattles, squeaky toys, and shakers. Show her how to use them, and then allow her to let loose.

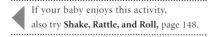

If your baby enjoys this activity, also try **Shake, Rattle, and Roll,** page 148.

A BABY BECOMES her own rhythm section as soon as she gets some simple musical toys.

6 MONTHS AND UP

TOTALLY TUBULAR

SKILLSPOTLIGHT

Playing peekaboo with swim tubes lets babies experience a temporary visual separation from you, which will eventually help them understand that even if you leave, you haven't disappeared forever. Crawling in, out, and over the rings lets babies practice being mobile on an uneven surface, which helps them develop balance and coordination.

Balance	✔
Gross Motor Skills	✔
Object Permanence	✔

YOUR BABY may not have entered an ocean, a lake, or even a kiddie pool yet, but large swim tubes provide plenty of fun on dry land, too. Sitters and crawlers alike enjoy using the tubes for sitting support. Or play a game of peekaboo in the rings. Just sit her down in one on a soft surface, stack the rest of them up to her chest, and lift them off while calling "Peekaboo!" enthusiastically. Babies who are more mobile will take pleasure in creeping and crawling in and out of several tubes placed on the floor.

If your baby enjoys this activity, also try **Cushion Mountain,** page 182.

STACK THEM UP and let the fun begin. You can play all sorts of baby games with a set of swim tubes.

6 MONTHS
6
AND UP

163

CLAPPING SONGS

AS YOUR BABY'S MANUAL DEXTERITY improves, she'll become fascinated with hand movements like clapping, finger snapping, and hand waving. Amplify her delight by singing songs that incorporate simple gestures. While she won't be able to perform each movement, eventually she'll learn to clap or wave. Coax her along by clapping or waving her hands for her, or clapping and waving yourself.

BINGO

There was a farmer had a dog
and Bingo was his name-o
B-I-N-G-O
B-I-N-G-O
B-I-N-G-O
and Bingo was his name-o.

There was a farmer had a dog
and Bingo was his name-o
clap-**I-N-G-O**
clap-**I-N-G-O**
clap-**I-N-G-O**
and Bingo was his name-o.
keep adding one clap and removing
one letter

WORKING ON THE RAILROAD

I've been working on the railroad
all the live-long day.
make digging motions with hands

I've been working on the railroad
just to pass the time away.
Can't you hear the whistle blowin'?
"pull" an imaginary whistle string

Rise up so early in the morn.
raise hands into air

Can't you hear the captain shouting,
clap

"Dinah, blow your horn."

THIS OLD MAN

clap out rhythm throughout

**This old man, he played one,
he played knick knack on my thumb,
with a knick, knack, paddy whack,
give a dog a bone;
this old man went rolling home.**

**This old man, he played two,
he played knick knack on my shoe,
with a knick, knack, paddy whack,
give a dog a bone;
this old man went rolling home.**

*continue with additional verses:
three/knee, four/door, five/hive,
six/sticks, seven/up in heaven,
eight/gate, nine/spine, and
ten/once again*

WHETHER YOU'RE MAKING the movement
for her or she's making elementary motions
herself, putting words, music, and
gestures together helps build
your baby's vocabulary.

SPOTLIGHT

SKILL SPOTLIGHT

Watching the light dance across the ceiling, walls, and toys strengthens your baby's ability to visually track objects. Seeing the light disappear and reappear over and over will delight her.

Fine Motor Skills	✔
Sensory Development	✔
Visual Development	✔

PEN YOUR BABY'S EYES to something new by putting on a light show for her. Just stretch brightly colored tissue paper or a sheer scarf across a flashlight and attach it firmly with masking tape or a rubber band (make sure your baby can't get the rubber band). Then shine the colored circle across the ceiling, on your baby's toys, and on the walls. Try turning the light on and off quickly, drawing shapes with the beam, or moving the light slowly back and forth between two objects. Talk to her as you play, saying, "Where did the light go? Oh, there it is! It's on the ball."

If your baby enjoys this activity, also try **Magic Scarves,** page 172.

AREAS OF BRIGHT LIGHT are exciting, especially when they shine on toes and toys.

LITTLE DRUMMER BABY

SKILL SPOTLIGHT

At this age, babies start to get a very elementary understanding of cause and effect. Hitting an object and having it make noise reinforces that concept while strengthening the baby's eye-hand coordination. And hearing the different sounds that various objects make helps him learn about the properties of those objects, which he'll later transfer to other situations.

BEING ABLE TO MANIPULATE OBJECTS is very gratifying for young babies who are working on fine motor control; being able to make noises with those objects is even more so. You can easily entertain your baby by setting up pots, pans, and bowls near him and providing him with wooden spoons. Show your baby how to hit the "drums" to make a noise, then encourage him to try it himself. He may hit the pots accidentally, which will give him enough of a taste to start tapping them on purpose.

Cause and Effect	✔
Eye-Hand Coordination	✔
Listening	✔

If your baby enjoys this activity, also try **Music Maker**, page 160.

A RAT-A-TAT-TAT and a sis-boom-bang...
this elementary drum set introduces him
to the joys of noise, as well as to the idea
that his actions influence his world.

6 MONTHS
6
AND UP

FINGERPUPPET FUN

MAGIC AT YOUR FINGERTIPS

SKILLSPOTLIGHT

Listening to the puppets talk and sing will help your baby learn the art of conversation—that is, that first one person (or puppet, as the case may be) talks, and then the other person responds. Being tickled and nuzzled by his little friends provides both entertaining tactile stimulation and fun, positive interaction with you.

MESMERIZED BY MOTION and enchanted by animal toys, babies are natural audiences for a miniature puppet show. Slip on a fingerpuppet or two and let them bob, dance, kiss, tickle, and talk to your littlest spectator. At this age, he's likely to reach out, grab a puppet, and put it in his mouth, which is fine. (Just be sure the puppets have no small parts that can be pulled off and swallowed.) He's equally likely to babble, gurgle, and blow raspberries at the animated actors. You can also find a song to go with your puppet and make it a musical show!

| Social Development | ✔ |
| Tactile Stimulation | ✔ |

If your baby enjoys this activity, also try **I'm Gonna Get You,** page 194. ▶

A PERKY PURPLE MOUSE gives him someone new to babble with.

MAGIC SCARVES

SKILL SPOTLIGHT

Grabbing the silky scarf and pulling it from the tube lets your baby work on his eye-hand coordination along with his fine motor skills. And seeing the scarf first disappear and then reappear at the other end will boost your baby's understanding of object permanence.

MAKING YOUR OWN

If you don't have any scarves lying around, you can buy colorful squares of cloth at fabric or novelty stores. Empty facial tissue boxes can replace the cardboard tube—show your baby how to stuff the scarf in and pull it out!

I F   Y O U ' R E   L O O K I N G for a versatile toy that will last through several of your child's developmental stages, you need look no further than your clothes closet. Old scarves—the silky kind—can delight and entertain him up through his preschool years. When he's still a baby, one of the best games you can play is to poke a scarf through one end of a cardboard tube and let him pull it out the other side. You can play the game without the tube by hiding most of the scarf in your fist and letting him find and grab the end. Embellish the game by adding your own enticements— "Where's the scarf? Where did it go? Oh, there it is. Peekaboo!"—to help keep him engaged.

Eye-Hand Coordination	✔
Object Permanence	✔
Tactile Stimulation	✔

If your baby enjoys this activity, also try **Busy Boxes,** page 176.

SOMETIMES IT TAKES nothing more than a cardboard tube, a colorful scarf, and Mommy's time to put a baby on cloud nine.

STOP THE TOP

SKILL SPOTLIGHT

Touching an object that's just lying there, like a block, is one challenge. Tracking and touching an object that's moving is a completely different challenge—one that this activity lets your baby practice over and over again. In addition, seeing how a gentle touch can either stop the spinning top or send it careening across the floor teaches your baby valuable lessons about cause and effect.

Cause and Effect	✔
Eye-Hand Coordination	✔
Spatial Awareness	✔

A SPINNING TOP is one of those old-fashioned toys that can delight all kinds of babies. Small babies obviously can't pump the handle up and down, but that doesn't mean they have to be passive observers. Instead, make the top spin in front of your baby. Then show him how to stop it by touching it with your hand. He'll soon start reaching out with his hands to control the whirling colors and whirring noises himself.

If your baby enjoys this activity, also try **Get That Bubble,** page 158.

174

ENCHANT YOUR CHILD with the
dazzling colors of a spinning top.

175

BUSY BOXES

LITTLE TASKS FOR LITTLE FINGERS

SKILLSPOTLIGHT

Even the simplest activities help a baby develop finger dexterity and coordination, which leads to more advanced tasks in later months. Learning that touching different knobs creates different results helps her mentally classify those results, and also builds upon her sense of mastery.

Cause and Effect	✔
Eye-Hand Coordination	✔
Fine Motor Skills	✔

OLD-FASHIONED ACTIVITY BOARDS with cylinders that whirl, dials that spin, and buttons that squeak can provide hours of amusement for your baby's curious fingers. Just set up the board so she can reach all the "stations," and show her how it works. Then let her try her own hand at it. At first, she may be able to do only the very simplest activities on the board, such as sticking her finger in a hole on the dial or swatting a rolling ball. In the months to come, though, she'll learn to spin the dial and make all of the buttons squeak and move.

If your baby enjoys this activity, also try **Pop-Up Play,** page 192.

YOU'LL PIQUE her curiosity and keep her fingers busy with one of these classic baby toys.

177

SEPARATION ANXIETY

JUST WHEN your baby is gaining a good deal of mobility and a tiny bit of independence, he suddenly wants to be joined to your hip once again. Your baby's newfound independence and his newly expressed separation anxiety are related. Now that he's mobile, he also understands how easily the two of you can become separated.

Knowing that your presence means so much can feel very flattering, but it can also fray your nerves. Here are some tips that can help you get through this challenging period.

Respect him: Remember that your presence is still essential to your baby, and he can't help being distraught at the thought that you're not there.

Reassure him: Hold him, talk to him, sing to him, and once he calms down, distract him by giving him a book or toy. Reassurance now will help him feel more secure later.

Protect him: Separation anxiety and stranger anxiety often arrive hand in hand. If strangers get too close, explain that your baby's not comfortable around new people and let him hide on your shoulder. Don't scold him for being shy; he can't help it. Given time, most babies will warm up to new people who are friendly and gentle in their approach.

Tell him the truth: It's tempting to try to slip out the back door when you have to leave him with a caregiver, but that won't help your baby. If he thinks that you really do suddenly disappear from time to time, he's more likely to panic if you step out of the room. Be cheerful and clear when you announce your departure, tell him you love him, and walk out the door. If he learns that he can trust you to be truthful and that you really will return, he'll feel more confident.

Remember that it's not forever: Infants, toddlers, and preschoolers all go through stages of separation anxiety. Given comfort, love, and encouragement, most children become quite independent over time. ■

ROLY-POLY

Roly-Poly

Roly-poly, roly-poly,
circle arms around one another
(repeat whenever singing roly-poly)
out, out, out.
move hands away from each other
Roly-poly, roly-poly,
in, in, in.
bring hands together
Roly-poly, roly-poly,
touch your nose.
touch baby's nose
Roly-poly, roly-poly,
touch your toes.
pull baby to seated position
Roly-poly, roly-poly,
up to sky.
pull baby up to standing
Roly-poly, roly-poly,
fly, fly, fly.
lift baby up into the air

Gross Motor Skills	✔
Language Development	✔
Lower-Body Strength	✔

YOUR BABY has probably enjoyed rocking and even standing supported in your lap since she was just a few months old. Now that her muscles are getting stronger, she'll be even more motivated to stand on her own two feet with your assistance. Make practice fun by accompanying it with a merry movement chant (see the lyrics at left). Start by laying your baby down on her back so that she's facing you with her legs out straight. Then gently help her to sit and stand as you engage in this roly-poly activity.

If your baby enjoys this activity, also try **Little Folks' Songs,** page 184.

SHE'S STANDING, she's learning words, and best of all, you and she are looking right at each other as you play.

CUSHION MOUNTAIN

SKILL SPOTLIGHT

Your baby needs to apply his crawling technique, in which he alternates his hands and legs, to climb a vertical surface. That requires a good amount of coordination, strength, and balance. But when he gets it, he'll be on his way to the challenges of jungle gyms, steep dirt mounds, and playground ladders.

Balance	✔
Bilateral Coordination	✔
Gross Motor Skills	✔
Upper-Body Strength	✔

LEARNING TO CRAWL will fill your little one with great glee. And once he's mastered moving horizontally on all fours, he's ready to try his hand at climbing. Just pile some cushions on the floor and show him how to clamber across them. Before long the squishy terrain and vertical challenge will have him smiling.

• Not all babies will climb a cushion mountain just because it's there. Try placing a new or favorite toy on top of the cushions to entice your baby to venture forth.

• Incorporating a rousing game of peekaboo may also instill courage in an uncertain baby. Hide yourself behind one cushion and encourage your baby to come across the others to find you. A proficient crawler may also enjoy a good game of "I'm Gonna Get You" (see page 194), in which you gently chase him over the cushiony peaks.

HE'LL GO OVER THE MOUNTAIN to see what he can see, if you're right there with him—and if the mountain is made of cushions.

RESEARCH REPORT

Wondering how much judgment your newly mobile baby has? One study of crawling babies found that most wouldn't cross a sheet of Plexiglas laid over a sharp drop, even if their mothers were coaxing them. But when the babies attempted to turn around, they inadvertently moved their center of gravity over the drop, which would have resulted in a bad fall if there had been no Plexiglas there. In other words, although babies show some judgment (that is, they're cautious about falling), there are still some gaps in their cognitive awareness and physical abilities.

LITTLE FOLKS' SONGS

S **URE,** children's television programs and videos provide lots of new songs for little kids. But sometimes it's the old songs that have the most charm, as they help knit generations together. Engage your child by singing these songs with our suggested hand gestures, and invite the whole family to join in!

DAISY, DAISY

Daisy, Daisy,
give me your answer, do.
clap hands together

I'm half-crazy
over the love of you.
put hands on baby's cheeks

It won't be a fancy marriage—
I can't afford a carriage.
shrug shoulders with hands turned up

But you'll look sweet upon the seat
point at baby

of a bicycle built for two.
hug baby

IT'S RAINING, IT'S POURING

It's raining, it's pouring,
the old man is snoring.
He bumped his head,
and fell out of bed,
and couldn't get up
in the morning.

RAIN, RAIN, GO AWAY

Rain, rain, go away,
come again some other day.
Rain, rain, go away,
all the children want to play.

POLLY WOLLY DOODLE

**Oh I went down South for
to see my Sal,
sing Polly Wolly Doodle all the day.**
tickle baby under chin or ribs

**My Sal she is a spunky gal,
sing Polly Wolly Doodle all the day.**
tickle baby under chin or ribs

Fare thee well,
wave bye-bye

fare thee well,
wave bye-bye

fare thee well my fairy Faye.
wave bye-bye

For I'm going to Louisiana
run fingers up and down baby's body

**for to see my Susyanna,
sing Polly Wolly Doodle
all the day.**
tickle baby under ribs

HEY DIDDLE DIDDLE

**Hey diddle diddle, the cat and
the fiddle,**
make fiddling motion with hands

the cow jumped over the moon.
sail hand through the air

**The little dog laughed to see
such a sight**
put hands over eyes

**and the dish ran away
with the spoon.**
run fingers from baby's belly to chin

MOMMY'S LAP offers the perfect
place for your baby to perch
while listening to favorite songs.

WHERE'S THE TOY?

SKILL SPOTLIGHT

Learning that something exists even when she can't see it helps your baby understand the concept of object permanence. This is key to her ability to tolerate separations from you, as well as to remember people, places, or objects she saw previously but that are currently out of sight. This ability is called "representational memory."

Fine Motor Skills	✔
Object Permanence	✔

WHEN SHE WAS JUST A LITTLE BABY, your child was very much an "out of sight, out of mind" type of creature. That is, if you hid a toy from her, she figured it no longer existed. But now that she's reached the six-month threshold, she's on to better ideas. While she may not know exactly where the toy went or why it disappeared, she understands that it still exists, somewhere, at least for a little while. You can bolster her understanding of this very basic fact by playing "peekaboo" games with toys.

• Partially hide a favorite plush toy or book under one of her blankets. Ask her repeatedly, "Where is it?" She may need some help finding it the first time, but once she realizes that the rest of the toy is connected to the part that's showing, she'll be diving into the blanket with joy.

• Soon you can begin hiding the toy completely. As long as your baby sees you hide it or notices the toy's outline beneath the blanket, she should be able to find it.

NOW IT'S HERE, now it's gone... even a blanket and a toy can teach little ones important lessons about object permanence—and fun.

RESEARCH REPORT

Only a few short months ago, your baby was still experiencing the jerks, twitches, and funny mouth movements associated with newborn reflexes. Now she's sitting up, kicking her legs, and yanking a blanket off her plush toy. What happened? Those first reflexes, like breathing and the heartbeat, originated in your baby's brain stem, which is fully mature at birth. But between four and seven months, her cortex, which governs motor movements, develops and allows motor skills to blossom.

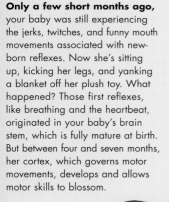

187

BABY'S CUPBOARD

SKILL SPOTLIGHT

Shelves full of tempting "toys" help your baby practice her "aim and fire" technique—that is, her ability to see an object, reach for it, and grab it. Having a variety of objects to manipulate lets your baby learn more about physical properties such as size, shape, and weight. It also gives her a chance to explore and discover safe items on her own terms.

Fine Motor Skills	✔
Gross Motor Skills	✔
Sensory Development	✔
Visual Discrimination	✔

NOW THAT YOUR BABY'S getting mobile, it's crucial that you babyproof any cupboards containing breakables, cleaning products, heavy pots and pans, or other materials that could harm her. But if she sees you taking things out of cupboards, it's guaranteed she'll want to do the same—grabbing games, like clearing shelves and emptying cupboards, are favorite pastimes of babies this age. You can keep your baby safe while satisfying her urge to explore and imitate by devoting a cupboard especially to her. An unlocked cabinet stocked with safe, appealing objects such as towels, plastic bowls, measuring cups, muffin tins, and a few favorite toys will keep her happily occupied—and it will give you some time to focus on cooking, washing dishes, or even reading a newspaper or magazine!

BABY'S "WORKING" in the kitchen just like you, but she's not getting into trouble, or even making a mess!

189

SAND MAN

Sand play delivers many benefits, including letting your baby practice his fine motor skills (pouring and digging with a shovel, spoon, or his fingers), allowing him to explore the properties of items such as sand or cornmeal, and introducing him to concepts like full, empty, heavy, light, and even "uh-oh" (when he spills the sand out of the box).

Fine Motor Skills	✔
Gross Motor Skills	✔
Tactile Stimulation	✔

AT SIX MONTHS you can introduce your baby to the pleasures of sand play—even if the weather is bad or a large sandbox isn't readily available. Just create a miniature sandbox. Set up a big dishpan outside or on newspapers indoors (to contain the overflow). Fill the pan with clean sand (available at toy stores) or coarse cornmeal, and provide your baby with shovels, plastic cups, wooden spoons, and any other tools you think he can use. Then let him explore to his heart's content. He may try to eat the sand, but he will enjoy the feel of it between his fingers even more!

If your baby enjoys this activity, also try **Dumping Delights,** page 150.

PLAYING WITH SAND is a game that provides many different kinds of fun—especially when shared with a parent or another child.

6 MONTHS AND UP

POP-UP PLAY

SKILL SPOTLIGHT

Being able to make a character disappear is enormously satisfying for babies who are learning about the concept of object permanence and experiencing separation anxiety, because it puts them in control of the separation. Learning to first push the animals down and then make them pop up again also lets your baby exercise his fine motor skills and develop his understanding of cause and effect.

Cause and Effect	✔
Eye-Hand Coordination	✔
Fine Motor Skills	✔
Object Permanence	✔

POP-UP TOYS with characters that burst out of a "hatch" when a button is pushed provide endless fun for babies who are working on fine motor skills. Granted, your baby may initially only be able to squish the characters back down while you work the buttons that bring them popping up again. Don't worry, that's plenty of stimulation for your little one. And before long he'll learn how to flip switches, turn keys, and press the more difficult buttons to make the animals reappear all by himself.

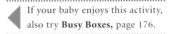

If your baby enjoys this activity, also try **Busy Boxes,** page 176.

"WHERE'S THE PANDA? Oh, there it is—and I'm the one who made it come up!" Pop-up boards let kids play peekaboo even when there's no adult to join in the game.

193

I'M GONNA GET YOU

AN OLD-FASHIONED GAME OF CHASE

SKILL SPOTLIGHT

This is a game for two to play, and it can help build your baby's social awareness as well as his sense of trust. Having an incentive to crawl also strengthens his balance and gross motor skills.

Balance	✔
Gross Motor Skills	✔
Social Development	✔
Trust	✔

N O ONE REALLY KNOWS why babies love to be chased. Even most early crawlers seem to think that having a parent or beloved caretaker thundering along after them is very, very funny.

• Start crawling slowly after your baby, murmuring "I'm gonna get you…I'm gonna get you…I'm gonna get you!" Then gently grab your baby and say, "I got you!" You can lift him up in the air, kiss the nape of his neck, and give his ribs a little tickle, but keep the game gentle so you don't startle him too much—he's still a baby, after all.

• A good game of chase isn't just for crawlers; it will keep him on his toes as a toddler and eventually evolve into classic big-kid games like hide-and-seek and tag.

A GENTLE GAME OF CHASE teaches him that Mom can be fun and boisterous as well as cuddly and calm. This helps him understand the range of social behavior humans can show.

RESEARCH REPORT

You may have noticed that you don't have to start a full-blown game of chase to make your baby squeal with delight. Just the beginning of your special "I'm gonna get you" growly voice can make him giggle. That's because even at this age his memory has developed enough for him to remember what's coming next.

Does that mean he'll remember your chase style when he's a teenager? That's debatable. For years, researchers believed that events experienced before the development of language couldn't be accessed. But recent research shows that one- and two-year-olds can recall events from the first year if they're elicited correctly. That means that as a toddler, at least, your child may still appreciate your earlier efforts, even if he can't verbally describe them.

195

BOTTLE ROLL

SKILLSPOTLIGHT

Encouraging your baby to grab a rolling bottle will likely motivate him to crawl after it, thereby exercising his gross motor skills. If he prefers to just sit and roll the bottle back and forth, he'll still be working on his fine motor skills as well as his eye-hand coordination.

Eye-Hand Coordination	✔
Fine Motor Skills	✔
Gross Motor Skills	✔

IT'S OK if your baby starts crawling later than the baby next door—they'll both be running and climbing with abandon in just a few short years. But if you'd like to coax a late or not very enthusiastic crawler into moving a bit more, a baby bottle filled with beans or grains can be an enticing lure. Just fill the bottle partially (so the contents can move) and roll it across the floor in front of your baby. Make sure the bottle top is safely secured. He still won't budge? Show him how to roll it back and forth himself, so he sees that it can provide plenty of sitting entertainment.

◀ If your baby enjoys this activity, also try **Play Ball**, page 156.

196

GO GET 'EM! He'll love to watch, listen to, and chase after these rolling bottles.

197

9 MONTHS AND UP

HOW PUZZLING!

FINDING THE RIGHT FIT

Playing with a puzzle (even getting the pieces out) is great exercise for a baby's fine motor and spatial skills. And learning which piece goes where draws on both her visual memory and her elementary understanding of shapes, sizes, and colors.

Fine Motor Skills	✓
Problem Solving	✓
Size and Shape Discrimination	✓
Visual Discrimination	✓

ASSEMBLING A JIGSAW PUZZLE is beyond your baby's reach, but she can easily grasp the concept behind the simple wooden puzzles made for older babies and toddlers. Those that feature simple shapes and large pieces with knobs are especially easy, as are those that have matching pictures underneath. There's a knack to getting even these big puzzle pieces in their places, however—you will probably need to guide the pieces as she moves them, so she can feel how they slip into place.

If your baby enjoys this activity, also try **Boxed Set,** page 236.

BIG WOODEN PUZZLE PIECES with colorful pictures are pleasing to the eye and help a baby learn about shapes and sizes.

BABY SOCCER

Swinging your baby's legs can help strengthen her abdominal and leg muscles. And feeling the ball on her legs and feet gives her greater body awareness. She's also tracking an object while she's in motion, which stands her in good stead when it comes time for her to kick a ball as a toddler.

Eye-Foot Coordination	✔
Gross Motor Skills	✔
Social Skills	✔

YOUR BABY WON'T LEARN how to kick a ball on the ground until she's in her second year, but even a nine-month-old can play a rousing game of baby soccer if you provide the muscle power. Pick her up under her arms and swing her legs at a lightweight, medium-sized ball. The position of her body and legs combined with the momentum you provide will make the ball roll across the floor or yard. No need to keep this game all to yourselves. Older siblings can join the action, or you can play with another adult-baby "team." The more, the merrier!

WHEN BIG BROTHER is the goalie, everyone has a ball!

SOUND STAGE

Focused listening builds the foundation for your child's language development. It allows him to locate and recognize sounds, and when combined with other experiences and repetition, he begins to form a repertoire of receptive language.

Language Development	✔
Listening	✔
Sensory Development	✔
Social Skills	✔

NOT ALL OF YOUR TIME with your baby needs to be spent talking, playing, reading, or otherwise stimulating his little mind. Just sitting and observing the obvious can also build sensory and cognitive awareness. One listening exercise, for instance, is as simple as finding an area where your baby can hear a number of different sounds. It may be inside, where he can hear the dog's toenails clicking on the kitchen floor, the refrigerator running, the telephone ringing, or cars zooming by. Or it may be outside, where he can hear birds singing, leaves rustling, a wind chime jingling, or an airplane overhead. Call his attention to the sounds, point in the right direction, and tell him what they are. You can let him participate in making the sounds by hitting the wind chimes or encourage him to imitate the sounds—the "tweet-tweet" of a bird, for instance, or the "vrooom" of a car driving by the house.

If your baby enjoys this activity, also try **Let's Explore,** page 210.

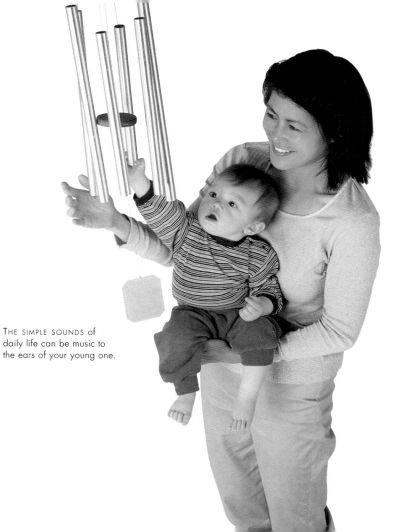

THE SIMPLE SOUNDS of daily life can be music to the ears of your young one.

TRAVELING WITH BABY

BY THE TIME your child is nine months old, life at home has probably settled a bit. You've bonded with your baby, your home is somewhat childproof, and you know how to keep him entertained and safe throughout the day.

But once you leave the comforts of home, life with a baby this age can be unsettling. While a very young baby can sleep through plane changes and family reunions, an older baby has more distinct wants and needs and is less likely to go with the flow.

Does that mean you should avoid travel until your baby is an adolescent? Not at all. Families need to take vacations, and most relatives will relish a visit from you. The trick is to expect the best outcomes but plan for potential obstacles.

Remember his schedule: Planning your travel schedule around your baby's sleep times can help you avoid the stress of dealing with a tired baby once you reach your destination. Throughout your trip, remember that the more rested he is, the more fun your whole family will have.

Remember his important items: If your baby has a stuffed toy or blanket that he uses for comfort, be sure to bring it. Familiar things help to ease the transition to a new environment.

Remember his food: In a hotel or a friend's kitchen, it won't be as easy to whip up his favorite snack. Carry foods like crackers, dry cereal, and fruit, and do a quick shopping trip when you arrive so that you have the food you need on hand.

Remember to babyproof: You won't be able to relax if you're worried about his safety. Pack a few outlet plugs and cupboard locks.

Remember your needs: Travel is tiring even when you don't have a baby. Try to eat and sleep well and get some exercise. You can get precious time to yourself by asking a relative to watch your child or by hiring a recommended local sitter. ■

BEEP-BEEP

SKILL SPOTLIGHT

Most babies won't figure out how to use their legs alternately on a riding toy until their second year. But as they move themselves forward and backward with both feet at once, they build gross motor skills and improve their balance.

Balance	✔
Gross Motor Skills	✔
Lower-Body Strength	✔

SOMETIMES IT'S HARD TO KNOW when to introduce certain toys, because it's hard to know how skilled a baby needs to be to use them. But even a baby who isn't yet walking can use a riding toy, as long as her legs are long enough to reach the ground. At first you may have to push her a bit so she understands what this game is all about. But soon she'll be pushing herself along (although, as with crawling, she may go backward at first), and squealing delightedly as she rolls from room to room.

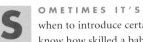

If your baby enjoys this activity, also try **Push Me, Pull You,** page 246.

YOUR CHILD'S FIRST RIDING TOY acquaints her with the delights of independent mobility—and riding it is really good exercise!

9 MONTHS AND UP

209

LET'S EXPLORE

SKILLSPOTLIGHT

It's easy for adults to take our daily environment for granted. After all, we've been seeing and hearing it every day for years. But babies are greatly intrigued—and their brains stimulated—by new sights and sounds, and just about everything in your world is still new to them. Encouraging your baby to explore the world with her senses, even if it's from the safety of your arms, helps teach her to be actively curious. Your narration also helps build her vocabulary.

Eye-Hand Coordination	✔
Listening	✔
Sensory Development	✔
Visual Development	✔

AT THIS AGE, your baby's curiosity about the world around her far exceeds her ability to explore it—even if she is already walking. Give her a lift toward making her first great discoveries by taking her around and describing the local sights.

• Inside the house, show her paintings, posters, books, knobs, and light switches. Let her work the light switch, pull a towel off the rack, or grab a toothbrush from its holder. Describe what she sees and touches—the nubby peel of an orange, for instance, or the soft towel in her hand.

• Take her outside and let her feel the bark of a tree, the leaves on a shrub, or the warmth of a stone in the sun. Lift her up to smell the blossoms on an apple tree or to meet a kitten by the window.

• Don't be surprised if something odd catches her fancy. Most children like animals, but during this stage they also have an interest in inanimate objects, such as door hinges, stereo knobs, and push buttons, and are curious about how they work.

SHOWING HER the many different objects in our world and describing them introduces her to important textures, words, and concepts.

SEARCHLIGHT

SKILLSPOTLIGHT

Whether your baby is crawling or walking, trying to catch the colored light improves his eye-hand coordination and agility. Young walkers who chase after the beam of light also hone their balance and visual skills.

Balance	✔
Eye-Hand Coordination	✔
Gross Motor Skills	✔

INCREASED MOBILITY brings with it a whole new range of games that involve chasing and catching. Most of those games have you pursuing your baby. But he can play the pursuer when you show him how to "catch" a flashlight beam. Wrap and secure a layer of colored tissue paper around the end of a flashlight, shine the colored light on the floor, on the wall, or on low furniture, and encourage your baby to "go get it."

If your baby enjoys this activity, also try **Spotlight,** page 166.

FOLLOWING THE CIRCLE of colorful light requires concentration and coordination.

OBSTACLE COURSE

SKILLSPOTLIGHT

Whether your child is crawling or already tottering along without holding on, negotiating an obstacle course helps her learn how to keep her balance. It also helps her develop eye-foot coordination as she practices lifting her feet and putting them in a "safe" spot.

Balance	✔
Eye-Foot Coordination	✔
Gross Motor Skills	✔
Lower-Body Strength	✔

WALKING ON A FLAT SURFACE is one challenge; crawling around or stepping over things while upright is another—and it's an important skill for a baby who's learning to maneuver through a sandbox, near household pets, or over the roots of a tree in the backyard. Help your baby learn to navigate around objects on the ground by setting up a series of small blocks, boxes, and plush toys. If she's walking, hold her hands and help her step over the objects. If she's crawling, encourage her to crawl around this makeshift obstacle course.

If your baby enjoys this activity, also try **Upstairs, Downstairs,** page 250.

MASTERING THE CHALLENGE of stepping over objects can boost her self-esteem and walking skills.

9 MONTHS AND UP

215

NOTHING IS MORE COMPELLING
than doing what big brother does.

I CAN DO IT, TOO!

AT NINE MONTHS, your baby may already be imitating you by swiping at the floor when you're cleaning or by waving a wooden spoon at a bowl as you cook. Encourage her interest in the adult world by giving her baby-sized versions of adult tools like brooms, mops, toolboxes, toy shopping carts, and strollers. If she's walking, you can show her how to take the stuffed dog for a stroller ride. She may not have great coordination at this age, but these are her very first explorations of what will become pretend-play, a realm that will engage her increasingly in her toddler and preschool years.

If your baby enjoys this activity, also try **Monkey See**, page 248.

SKILL SPOTLIGHT

Learning how to put a plush toy in a stroller, how to handle a broom, and how to stir with a plastic spoon helps your baby gain a better sense of spatial relations and develops her fine motor skills. Equally important is the opportunity to mimic what the big kids and adults in her world are doing.

✔	**Fine Motor Skills**
✔	**Social Skills**
✔	**Spatial Awareness**

ZANY XYLOPHONES

SKILLSPOTLIGHT

Learning how to hear different notes, and eventually to associate them with different keys, helps your baby develop her listening skills. Gaining the skill to hit the keys one by one helps her develop eye-hand coordination and fine motor skills. And learning that she, too, can make music builds self-esteem.

Eye-Hand Coordination	✔
Fine Motor Skills	✔
Listening	✔

YOUR BABY'S MUSICAL PURSUITS needn't be limited to baby stuff like rattles, bells, and windup toys. A simple xylophone designed for children under three years of age (available in music and toy stores) allows her to bang out a tune no matter where the mallet lands. It can also introduce her to the idea of musical scales if you show her how the notes go higher and lower when you play in different directions.

If your baby enjoys this activity, also try **Music Maker,** page 160.

YOUR BABY WILL LOVE to discover that different keys make different sounds.

POURING PRACTICE

SKILL SPOTLIGHT

When your baby was younger, he didn't have the coordination to handle most objects. Now he's capable not only of lifting objects but also of tipping and twisting them. This activity helps him work with his hands to develop fine motor skills. It also helps him practice his eye-hand coordination.

| Eye-Hand Coordination | ✔ |
| Fine Motor Skills | ✔ |

E MPTYING AND FILLING one container is fun; emptying stuff from one container into another is twice as much fun. It's also an easy game to set up. Just gather some plastic cups, bowls, and buckets, plus spoons or small shovels. Then add either water (in a small basin or in the tub), sand (in the sandbox), or cornmeal (at the kitchen table or in a high chair). Show your baby how to fill a cup, spoon, shovel, or bowl with one of the substances. Watch as he enjoys fingering the sand or cornmeal or splashing the water—exploring the textures and how the items work together. Then show your baby how to pour the sand, cornmeal, or water out again. Before long he'll figure out how first to fill a container, then empty it into another.

◀ If your baby enjoys this activity, also try **Sand Man,** page 190.

A STREAM OF SAND can be
fascinating to watch and also
teaches babies the concepts
of empty, full, fast, and slow.

ANIMAL SONGS

AT THIS AGE, most babies are beginning to notice the noises animals make and the ways they move. That means it's a good age to introduce songs with funny animal sounds. Your baby will be intrigued by the words and melodies that will later become part of his regular repertoire.

WHERE, OH WHERE?

Oh where, oh where
has my little dog gone?
Oh where, oh where can he be?
With his ears so short
and his tail so long,
oh where, oh where can he be?

YOUR BABY WILL LOVE interacting with animal puppets while you sing silly animal songs.

SING A SONG OF SIXPENCE

Sing a song of sixpence,
a pocket full of rye,
four and twenty blackbirds,
baked in a pie.

When the pie was opened,
the birds began to sing.
What a dainty dish that was
to set before a king.

MARY HAD A LITTLE LAMB

Mary had a little lamb,
little lamb, little lamb,
Mary had a little lamb
whose fleece was
white as snow.

Everywhere that
Mary went,
Mary went,
Mary went,
everywhere that
Mary went,
that lamb was
sure to go.

OLD MACDONALD

Old MacDonald had a farm,
eee-i-eee-i-o.
And on his farm he had a dog,
eee-i-eee-i-o.
With a woof–woof here
and a woof–woof there,
here a woof, there a woof,
everywhere a woof–woof.
Old MacDonald had a farm,
eee-i-eee-i-o.
*continue the song, substituting other
animals and the sounds they make*

BATHING BEAUTY

SKILLSPOTLIGHT

Your baby's primary way of understanding her world is still through touch. This bath activity lets her soak up a whole new range of tactile stimuli as she explores different bathing tools.

Eye-Hand Coordination	✔
Fine Motor Skills	✔
Tactile Stimulation	✔

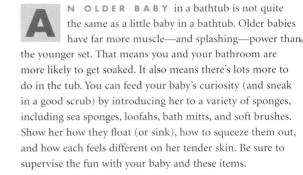

AN OLDER BABY in a bathtub is not quite the same as a little baby in a bathtub. Older babies have far more muscle—and splashing—power than the younger set. That means you and your bathroom are more likely to get soaked. It also means there's lots more to do in the tub. You can feed your baby's curiosity (and sneak in a good scrub) by introducing her to a variety of sponges, including sea sponges, loofahs, bath mitts, and soft brushes. Show her how they float (or sink), how to squeeze them out, and how each feels different on her tender skin. Be sure to supervise the fun with your baby and these items.

If your baby enjoys this activity, also try **Kick, Kick, Kick,** page 142.

YOUR BABY WILL LOVE the feel of all the different sponges while getting a good scrub!

225

9 MONTHS
9
AND UP

YOUR BABY'S MANUAL DEXTERITY,
word recognition, and social skills all
blossom when two play this game.

226

ACTIVITY BOOK

IS SHE TURNING BOOK PAGES, fiddling with clothing labels, and pulling ties off the tie rack? You can appeal to your baby's tinkering instinct by buying her an activity book or creating one from things found around your house. Just gather together pictures to look at (from magazines and postcards), textures to pat (cotton balls, fake fur, corduroy, crinkly tin foil, or bubble wrap), ribbons to tug, and old cards to open. You can securely glue them to pieces of cardboard and bind it all together with short pieces of ribbon.

If your baby enjoys this activity, also try **Friendly Faces,** page 102.

SKILL SPOTLIGHT

A book with cards to open, textures to feel, and pictures to peruse boosts your baby's budding fine motor skills. Your narration as she looks at the book—"There's the kitty," "This is soft," or "Can you open this?"—helps her learn both words and concepts.

✔ **Fine Motor Skills**

✔ **Language Development**

✔ **Tactile Stimulation**

KNOCKDOWN

SKILLSPOTLIGHT

Playing with towers of toys
helps babies develop both gross
and fine motor skills. Your baby
also has the opportunity to
explore spatial relationships and
differences in size and shape.

Fine Motor Skills	✔
Gross Motor Skills	✔
Size and Shape Discrimination	✔

A S OLDER BABIES gain greater hand and arm coordination, they often take great joy in placing one object on top of another. You can nurture this budding talent by building towers of blocks, books, cereal boxes, shoe boxes, or plastic bowls and cups for your baby. There are two steps to this fun for your baby: watching you stack the objects and then knocking them down herself.

If your baby enjoys this activity, also try **Boxed Set,** page 236.

KNOCKING DOWN the tower is only part of the experience. She is also learning about sizes and shapes.

229

STACKING RINGS

MAKING YOUR OWN

As an alternative to a premade stacking ring, take the cardboard tube from a roll of paper towels and some mason jar rings—or even rings cut from cardboard—and show your baby how to slide them on and off the tube.

SOME TOYS never go out of style. Good old-fashioned stacking rings are just as intriguing to babies today as they were to babies generations ago. You can buy wood or plastic sets, or make your own. A large set—made of bulky plastic rings, for instance—is usually easiest; older babies, with more advanced fine motor control, can tackle the sets with smaller poles.

• Start by showing your baby how to take the rings off—that's an easier task than fitting the rings over the pole. Don't be surprised if he simply picks up the toy, turns it upside down, and dumps the rings all over the floor. He's showing you the most obvious solution to the problem!

• Learning to stack the rings according to size—with the large ring on the bottom and the small ring on top—comes much later in the second year. In the meantime, let him practice getting the rings off and on the pole in any order.

BRIGHT COLORS, easy-to-handle rings, and some simple problems to solve keep babies motivated to stack the large rings again and again.

PUBLIC ETIQUETTE

YOUR BABY won't always smile and coo in public—even the happiest baby falls prey to fussiness. And the public won't always be receptive to a fussy baby. But you and your baby have to travel in public, even if it's just for a quick trip to the post office. Your life will be far easier if you learn how to cope with potential conflicts early on.

Countdown to meltdowns: A sure way to create a frustrated, crying baby is to haul her from place to place when she's tired, hungry, or sick. Solution? Don't do it. Try to keep errands short, do them when your baby is rested and well-fed, and bring a supply of books and toys for her to play with if you get stuck waiting.

Safeguard your privacy: Even mothers who felt perfectly comfortable nursing their newborn in public may feel a little bashful nursing an eleven-month-old in a shopping mall, especially if that eleven-month-old is walking and starting to talk. Strangers may give you funny looks for "still" nursing such a big baby. If this makes you uncomfortable and you find that you have to breast-feed in public, try to find a private corner where you and your baby can be alone and have some quiet time.

Protect against verbal assault: Blunt remarks about your baby can be annoying and hurtful. The best solution is for you to tactfully respond in a positive way. If someone at the grocery store declares that your baby boy is fat or mistakes him for a girl, you can reply with a very matter-of-fact "Yes, isn't he a gorgeous big boy?"

Part of the art of dealing with awkward public situations is displaying model behavior for your baby. He's not old enough to say "Please don't touch me" or "I'll outgrow my baby fat," but he is old enough to perceive how you deal with potential conflicts. Staying calm, matter-of-fact, and loving will teach him to behave the same way. ■

233

UH-OH!

SKILLSPOTLIGHT

Dropping things and watching them fall helps a baby learn about cause and effect. At this stage, your baby is also just beginning to understand that through her actions she can exert control over others—something she will test more and more as she gets older.

Cause and Effect	✔
Eye-Hand Coordination	✔
Grasp and Release	✔
Social Development	✔

IT'S A SIMPLE FACT that most older babies love to throw things from a higher perch—their high chair, grandma's lap, etc. Grownups can make this habit into a fun game by engaging the child when she is doing so. Place plastic cups, rattles, small plush toys, or blocks on the high-chair tray. Then sit on the floor next to the high chair and have the baby hand or toss the toys down to you. You can add to the fun by singing "uh-oh!" or "there it goes," or talking about how the toys go "down" and "up."

If your baby enjoys this activity, also try **Ball Drop,** page 238.

YOU CAN TURN her natural instinct to throw things into a fun learning game.

235

BOXED SET

SKILLSPOTLIGHT

A box and a lid provide an elementary kind of puzzle for a baby, as she has to figure out how to get the lid off (easy) and how to put it back on (harder). This task involves coordination and understanding the nature of both shapes and sizes. The activity also introduces her to the concepts of open, shut, full, empty, in, and out.

Fine Motor Skills	✓
Problem Solving	✓
Size and Shape Discrimination	✓
Spatial Awareness	✓

BOX OF WIPES, a bag of lentils, even the bowl of spaghetti left on the fridge's bottom shelf all fascinate your baby now. She wants to investigate everything in sight. You can safely keep her fingers busy by gathering a set of boxes with easy-to-manage tops (such as shoe boxes, empty diaper-wipe containers, and square gift boxes) and putting small toys and objects inside each. Say the words "open" or "closed" as she plays with the boxes and "in" and "out" as she plays with the toys.

If your baby enjoys this activity, also try **Pouring Practice,** page 220.

Empty boxes are fun to open and close; filled boxes are exciting to explore.

237

BALL DROP

BALLS, BOWLS, and anything that bangs are big hits with older babies. How can you get all those elements into one playtime? Just provide your baby with some lightweight balls (like whiffle or tennis balls) and a big metal bowl or plastic basket. Then show your baby how to drop the balls into the container. When the balls hit, they each make a different and interesting sound. Your baby will be intrigued by this simple activity and will gain an understanding of cause and effect.

DROPPING A BALL into a large bowl makes a great noise and improves eye-hand coordination.

SKILL SPOTLIGHT

Grabbing a ball comes pretty naturally to a baby after about the sixth month. Letting go of it again—as in a simple drop—is harder to learn, and intentionally throwing it is a future skill. This game lets your baby practice these first two skills while sharpening his eye-hand coordination.

✔ **Eye-Hand Coordination**

✔ **Fine Motor Skills**

✔ **Grasp and Release**

TUNNEL TIME

SKILLSPOTLIGHT

Crawling through small spaces
helps your baby learn just how big her body is in relation to other objects, which helps her develop both spatial and body awareness. This game also helps develop visual skills such as depth perception and builds her self-confidence as she maneuvers through the tunnel without the benefit of peripheral vision.

Body Awareness	✔
Gross Motor Skills	✔
Spatial Awareness	✔

EVER WONDER WHY your baby is so intent on wriggling under the bed, squeezing behind the couch, or curling up on the floor of your closet? A child this age is naturally intrigued with space—especially when it's just her size. You can cater to this fascination by providing a commercially made or cardboard tunnel for her to crawl through. Roll a ball down the tunnel and encourage her to go after it. Or put yourself or small toys, such as balls or beanbags, at the other end and coax her through.

SHE'S BOTH LEARNING about the nature of small spaces and enjoying the thrill of discovery when she crawls through a baby-sized tunnel.

RESEARCH REPORT

Educators have long believed that children exhibit distinct learning styles, or preferences, for taking in new information. Some kids need to physically explore something in order to understand it, while others need simply to see or hear it. Today some researchers believe that even infants show such preferences, as evidenced by their tendency to look at, listen to, or fiddle with objects very intently. Since babies need to develop all their senses, it's a good idea for parents to continue to offer their babies stimulating new environments to explore.

SING ABOUT ME

YOUR LITTLE ONE may not be able to say "mouth," "nose," "feet," or "toes," but he's probably already beginning to associate your spoken words with his body parts. You can boost his growing language and motor skills by teaching him these songs about the body. Gently move his arms and legs, and use your hands and fingers to indicate the parts of his body while you sing.

PAT-A-CAKE

Pat-a-cake, pat-a-cake, baker's man,
clap hands together

bake me a cake as fast as you can.
clap hands

Pat it and prick it,
tap finger on one palm

and mark it with a B,
trace an imaginary B on one palm

and put it in the oven for Baby and me.
pretend to slide a cake into an oven

NOSE, NOSE, JOLLY RED NOSE

Nose, nose, jolly red nose—
tap your own nose

and who gave thee that jolly red nose?
point to baby's nose

Nutmeg and ginger, cinnamon and cloves—
wrinkle up your nose and pretend to sniff your palm

that's what gave me this jolly red nose.
tap baby's nose

HERE ARE THE TOES

 to the *tune* of "Take Me Out to the Ball Game"

Here are the toes of my (baby's name),
tap on baby's toes

**here are the toes of my (gal/guy),
and here are his feet and
his tiny knees—**
tap on baby's feet and knees

**I can't help it—I'll give them
a squeeze.**
gently squeeze above baby's knees

**And he's got two arms
just for hugging,**
pat baby's arms

and hands that clap and wave.
clap baby's hands for him

**But it's his eyes, nose,
mouth, and chin**
tap baby's facial features

that really draw me in!
lean in and kiss baby's face

HEY MR. KNICKERBOCKER

**Hey Mr. Knickerbocker,
boppity-bop,**
*standing with your baby, rock him
from side to side*

**I sure like the way you
walkity walk.**
lean baby forward and back

**I like the way you
walkity walk
with your feet,
ch-ch-ch-ch-ch-ch-ch-ch-ch.**
walk forward

EYES, NOSE, FINGERS, and toes—your baby delights in Mommy's songs about him.

POPCORN, POPCORN

A BOUNCING-BALL GAME

Popcorn, Popcorn

Popcorn, popcorn,
sizzling in the pan.
Shake it up, shake it up,
bam bam bam.

Popcorn, popcorn,
now it's getting hot.
Shake it up, shake it up,
pop pop pop.

Cause and Effect ✔

Rhythm Exploration ✔

THERE'S NOTHING LIKE a bouncing ball to catch a baby's attention—and nothing like a waving blanket to make him giggle. You can combine these simple pleasures in the popcorn game. Take a blanket or bedsheet and have an older child assist you in holding the edges. Put some lightweight balls or a beach ball in the middle and shake the blanket first lightly, then more vigorously. The action of the balls popping into the air will delight your baby while teaching him about cause and effect.

• Adding a rhyming chant like "Popcorn, Popcorn" (see the lyrics at left) to the activity will help your baby gain a sense of rhythm.

THE BALL IS POPPING and so is the fun with this great group activity.

RESEARCH REPORT

All parents hope their children will be social and have plenty of friends, but it's not until a child's second year that he'll actively play with other children. Although your baby may be interested in looking at other babies, he may still crawl over them on the way to a desired toy or tap one of them on the head as a way to explore. Until he turns two, he'll engage primarily in "parallel play"—playing next to, but not with, other babies.

245

PUSH ME, PULL YOU

SKILL SPOTLIGHT

The support provided by a pushable object allows a baby to practice walking without holding on to furniture or your hands. By now, your baby has learned a little about how her body works—how she can work against gravity to keep herself upright as she moves forward. Walking and pushing help her develop balance and gross motor skills.

Balance	✔
Gross Motor Skills	✔
Lower-Body Strength	✔

I F YOUR BABY IS WALKING, or even starting to toddle, she will appreciate the support provided by a large object (like a push toy, stroller, or small chair) that she can push across the floor. A laundry basket filled with toys also makes a great walking aid. You might help her at first by pulling from the other side—but then watch out! She will soon want to do it all by herself.

A MOVABLE OBJECT that is just your baby's
size provides support but lets her feel like
she's walking all by herself.

MONKEY SEE

Just Like Me

 to the *tune* of "London Bridge Is Falling Down"

Make your hands go
clap clap clap,
clap clap clap,
clap clap clap.
Make your hands go
clap clap clap,
just like me.

Make your head go
side to side,
side to side,
side to side.
Make your head go
side to side,
just like me.

Body Awareness ✔

Language Development ✔

IMITATING OLDER PEOPLE— whether siblings, parents, or next-door neighbors—is a prime source of learning for an older baby, and you can turn that imitation instinct into a game. Slap your knees, bang the floor or high-chair tray, put your hands over your eyes, open your mouth wide, or tip your head from side to side as you sing a silly song. She'll learn new words for her body and its movements, and also discover the joy of an interactive game.

 If your baby enjoys this activity, also try **I Can Do It, Too!** page 216.

CREATING NEW SOUNDS while directing arm and finger movements helps your child develop auditory memory and rhythm.

UPSTAIRS, DOWNSTAIRS

SKILL SPOTLIGHT

Learning to reach his feet into a space he cannot see and then find firm footing teaches your baby a lot about spatial relations and balance. Stair practice also helps your baby develop a better sense of height and depth, which will make him more cautious in his future climbing pursuits.

Balance	✔
Gross Motor Skills	✔
Lower-Body Strength	✔
Spatial Awareness	✔

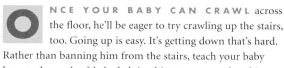

ONCE YOUR BABY CAN CRAWL across the floor, he'll be eager to try crawling up the stairs, too. Going up is easy. It's getting down that's hard. Rather than banning him from the stairs, teach your baby how to descend safely by helping him turn around on his belly—feet first—and find the stairs with his feet. Guidance is important at first. Use consistent cue words such as "turn around" or "feet first" each time your baby approaches the stairs. And don't let him head for the stairs on his own.

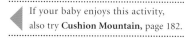

If your baby enjoys this activity, also try **Cushion Mountain,** page 182.

LEARNING HOW TO CLIMB and descend stairs safely is a crucial skill for all budding toddlers as well as a fun activity.

EVERY TODDLER-TO-BE relishes
the opportunity to cruise over
to a favorite toy.

252

MOVE IT ON OVER

SIMPLY MOVING from chair to chair, or from table to chair to magazine rack to Daddy's knee, provides plenty of fun for a baby who has discovered the pleasures of cruising. You can spice things up or inspire a baby who's not too sure how this cruising thing works by enticing her with hidden treasures along the way. Let her see you hide a favorite toy behind a cushion that's just beyond her grasp, or place it in view at the next stopover point. Then encourage her to get to the toy without resorting to crawling. The excitement of getting to the toy will help get her mind off her feet, which makes walking a lot easier.

If your baby enjoys this activity, also try **Tunnel Time,** page 240.

SKILL SPOTLIGHT

This easy activity stretches your baby's mind and body in several ways. It helps her develop the balance and gross motor skills necessary for cruising from one object to another. And it encourages her to figure out a way to get from one place to another—for example, from the coffee table to the sofa, where the toy is "hiding."

✔ **Balance**

✔ **Body Awareness**

✔ **Gross Motor Skills**

✔ **Lower-Body Strength**

GLOSSARY

A

AUDITORY DEVELOPMENT
The maturation of a child's hearing system, a necessary step in spoken language development.

B

BALANCE
The ability to assume and maintain body positions against the force of gravity. A sense of balance is crucial for learning how to roll over, sit, crawl, stand, walk, and run.

BILATERAL COORDINATION
The ability to use both sides of the body simultaneously, whether or not the movements are symmetrical. A child needs bilateral coordination to crawl, walk, swim, catch, climb, and jump.

BODY AWARENESS
A sense of how one's limbs, joints, and muscles work together and the ability to locate one's body parts without visual monitoring.

C

CAUSE AND EFFECT
How one action affects another. Experience with cause and effect helps a child learn how her actions create a result (when she drops the toy truck from the high chair, it falls on the floor).

COGNITION
Mental or intellectual abilities, including the ability to solve problems and remember routines, people, and object placement.

COGNITIVE DEVELOPMENT
A child's growing understanding and knowledge, and her developing ability to think and reason.

COORDINATION

The ability to integrate all of the senses to produce a movement response that is smooth, efficient, and skillful, such as reaching for and grasping a toy or another object.

E

EYE-FOOT COORDINATION

Gauging distance and depth with the eyes and processing that information to coordinate when and where to place the feet. Eye-foot coordination is required, for example, when kicking a target or walking on an uneven path.

EYE-HAND COORDINATION

Directing the position and motion of the hands in response to visual information, such as reaching out and grasping an offered toy.

F

FINE MOTOR SKILLS

Control of the small muscles, especially those in the hands, to execute small movements, such as picking up a raisin or plucking a blade of grass. This progresses to using tools such as spoons.

255

GLOSSARY

G

GRASP AND RELEASE
The ability to purposefully reach out and retrieve an object and subsequently to intentionally let the object go.

GROSS MOTOR SKILLS
Control of the large muscles, such as those in the arms and legs. Gross motor activities include crawling, walking, and running.

L

LANGUAGE DEVELOPMENT
The complex process of acquiring language skills including understanding human speech, producing sounds and spoken language, and eventually learning how to read and write.

LISTENING SKILLS
The ability to discern various sounds, including music, rhythm, pitch, and spoken language.

LOWER-BODY STRENGTH
The development of muscles in the legs and lower trunk. Such development is crucial to creeping, crawling, walking, and eventually running, skipping, and climbing.

O

OBJECT PERMANENCE
The concept that an object, or a person, that is no longer visible still exists.

P

PROBLEM SOLVING
The ability to work out a solution to a mental or physical puzzle. A child solves a problem when he figures out how to fit a piece into a puzzle, stack nesting boxes, or open a package.

R

RHYTHM EXPLORATION
The act of exploring the rhythms and underlying beat of music through movement.

ROLE-PLAYING
Mimicking others and eventually using imagination to pretend to be someone else.

S

SELF-CONCEPT
A child's understanding that he is an individual person separate from his parents.

SENSORY EXPLORATION
Using the senses—hearing, sight, smell, taste, and touch—to learn about the world.

SIZE AND SHAPE DISCRIMINATION
The ability to identify objects of different dimensions and their relationship to each other; for instance, nesting boxes or puzzle pieces and the spaces in which they fit.

GLOSSARY

SOCIAL DEVELOPMENT
A baby's growing understanding of her interactions with people and her influence on her world.

SOCIAL SKILLS
Interacting and relating to other people, including recognizing other people's emotions through their tone, actions, or facial expressions.

SPATIAL AWARENESS
Knowing where one's own body is in relation to other people and objects. For example, a child uses spatial awareness to crawl under a bed, crawl or walk between two pieces of furniture, and generally move through space.

T

TACTILE DISCRIMINATION
The ability to determine differences in shape or texture by touch. Being able to discern textures helps children explore and understand their environment and recognize objects.

TACTILE STIMULATION
Input to receptors that respond to pressure, temperature, and the movement of hairs on the skin. Tactile stimulation enables a child to feel

comfortable with new experiences such as first foods and unexpected touch.

TRUST
A child's belief in and reliance upon his parents (or others) to care for his basic needs.

U

UPPER-BODY STRENGTH
The development of muscles in the neck, shoulders, arms, and upper trunk. Such development is crucial to crawling, sitting, pulling oneself up, and walking.

V

VISUAL DEVELOPMENT
The maturation of a child's eyes and eyesight.

VISUAL DISCRIMINATION
The ability to focus on and distinguish objects within a visual field. A child uses visual discrimination to locate a bird in a picture, a desired stuffed animal in a toy chest, or even a parent in a crowd of people.

VISUAL MEMORY
The ability to recall objects, faces, and images. Visual memory allows a child to remember a sequence of objects or pictures and is a foundation for learning to read.

VISUAL TRACKING
The ability to follow the movement of an item by moving the eyes and rotating the head.

SKILLS INDEX

SKILLS INDEX

SKILLS INDEX

INDEX

INDEX

ACKNOWLEDGMENTS

A VERY SPECIAL ΓHANKS to all the children, parents, and grandparents featured in this book:

Tyler & Ashlynn Adams
Diane & Ashley Anderson
Greg, Denise &
   Aiden Ausley
Maiya Barsky
Dana & Robbie Bisconti
Whitney Boswell
Lizzie Boyle
Brynn & Riley Breuner
Danielle Bromley &
   Tyler Primas
Jackson Brooks
Chizzie & Patrick Brown
Millie Cervantes & Norma
   Foreman
Kailah Chavis
Tami & Averie Clifton
Katherine & Parker Cobbs
Kelly, Mark &
   Rebecca Cole
Bolaji, Kyle &
   Miles Davis
Jane & Lauren Davis
John & Jessica Davis
Justice Domingo
Elaine Doucet & Benjamin
   Martinez
Lauren Dunlap
Masooda & Sabrina Faizi
Quinn Folks
Shannon & Clayton Fritschi
Kristen Gilbert & Phenix

Dewhurst
Wendi & Joshua Gilbert
Patricia & Nathan Gilmore
Galen Gold
Alexa Grau
Candace Groskreutz & Matthew
   & Clare Colt
Walter, Ester & Whitney Hale
Danny & Yasmine Hamady
Ashley & Alyssa Hightower
Justin Hull
Margy Hutchinson & Isaiah
   Hammer
Katy & Logan Jaeger
Ryan Jahabli-Danekas
Stephanie Joe & Alexander &
   Isabelle Weiskopf
Elana Kalish
David & Giselle Kaneda
Ashley Kang
Esther Aliah Karpilow
Isabella Kearney
Thomas Keller
Sierra Kelly
Denise, Chloe & Ian Kidder
Jeff, Jennifer, Sydney,
   & Gunner Kinsey
Olivia Klein
Sonya Kosty-Bolt & Owen Bolt
Dan & Martin Krause
Isabelle Jubilee Kremer
Alicia & Devon Mandell

Lily Marcheschi
Kim & Miles Martinez
Beth & Alison Mason
Lisa & Zachary Mayor
Nathaniel McCarthy
Meredith & Sam McClintock
Jennifer, Jim & Abigail McManus
Maya & Jakob Michon
Sarah Miller & Elizabeth Schai
Kimberly Minasian & Isabelle
   Schulenburg
Mikayla Mooney
Nikolaus Moore
Theresa & Gabriel Moran
Mary, Jeff & Amanda Rose
   Morelli
Chantál & Kalle Myllymäki
Bodhi Nadalin
Sue, Katie & Christine
   Partington
Abigail Peach
Lori Pettegrew & Andrew Pike
Santiago Ponce
Bronwyn & Griffin Posynick
Ann Marie Ramirez & Damien
   Splan
Miles Reavis
Lynn Roff & Oliver Swede
Aliyah Ross
Lori, Mark & Zayle Rudiger
Renée Rylander & Ryan
   Ditmanson

Christine & Matthew Salah
Leigh & Kai Sata
Joseph Shin
Michelle Sinclair & Nicolas
   Amerkhanian
Colleen & Maxwell Smith
Nicole & Marlo Smith
Julia Stark
Denise & Adam Stenberg
Quincy Stivers
JoAnne Skinner Stott & Sonja
   Stott
Lori & Karl Strand
James & Jayson Summers
Sandi, Kimberly & Jacquelyn
   Svoboda
Michelle & Tatum Tai
Dylan Thompson
Rico & Deena Tolefree
Kathi & Lauren Torres
Annalisa & John "Jack" VanAken
Jim Vettel & Peyton Raab
Patty & Shawn Weichel
Molly & Jamie Wendt
Kathleen & Meredith Whalen
Emma Wong
Catherine Wood
Ajani Wright
Preeti & Shama Zalavadia
Allison Zanolli
Karen Zimmerman &
   Jarred Edgerly